INSPIRING COURAGE

Compose yourself
immerse yourself
in it. Erica ♡

We are pulling ♡
for you! Cheryl &
Bill Fogg

Kisses, head-bumps,
and snuggles from:
Razzle.
Chase.
Alfie.
Smooch.
Moxie.
Cubby.
& Grey Kitty ♥

A wonderful book by
a good friend of ours....
Barbara. We thought
you'd like a signed copy!
Here is to courage, to
faith, to strength and
most, most, most of all,
To LOVE.
And you are So Loved ♥
xoxo Ali

INSPIRING
COURAGE

BARBARA BONNER

Barbara Bonner (signature)

Wisdom

Wisdom Publications
199 Elm Street
Somerville, MA 02144 USA
wisdompubs.org

Library of Congress Cataloging-in-Publication Data
Names: Bonner, Barbara, 1948– author.
Title: Inspiring courage / Barbara Bonner.
Description: Somerville, MA : Wisdom Publications,
[2017] | Includes index.
Identifiers: LCCN 2016022005 (print) | LCCN
2016034122 (ebook) | ISBN
  9781614292616 (pbk. : alk. paper) | ISBN 1614292612
(pbk. : alk. paper) |
  ISBN 9781614292883 () | ISBN 1614292884 ()
Subjects: LCSH: Courage.
Classification: LCC BJ1533.C8 B55 2017 (print) | LCC
BJ1533.C8 (ebook) | DDC
  179/.6—dc23

LC record available at https://lccn.loc
.gov/2016022005

ISBN 978-1-61429-261-6
ebook ISBN 978-1-61429-288-3

21 20 19 18 17
5 4 3 2 1

Cover and Interior design by Gopa & Ted2, Inc.
Set in ITC Galliard Pro 10.5/16. Author photo by
Nancy Compton.

Wisdom Publications' books are printed on acid-free
paper and meet the guidelines for permanence and
durability of the Production Guidelines for Book
Longevity of the Council on Library Resources.

🌱 This book was produced with environmental
mindfulness. For more information, please visit
wisdompubs.org/wisdom-environment.

Printed in the
United States of America.

Please visit fscus.org.

For Archer and Nate:

May You Live Courageous Lives.

COURAGE
IS THE FIRST OF
HUMAN VIRTUES
BECAUSE IT MAKES ALL OTHERS
POSSIBLE. ARISTOTLE

Introduction

I**T TAKES COURAGE** to live a human life. We all have varying degrees of courage. For some, it is buried deep in hearts and psyches; for others, it is a bright light that guides every step. But, for all of us, finding courage can be a choice we make every day—often in the quietest of ways. There is great courage in living life to the fullest, living with authenticity and a sense of alignment with one's most deeply held values. And sometimes, simply getting up every day and putting one foot in front of the other is an act of immense courage.

This book is a collection of some of the most powerful inspirations I have encountered about what it means to live a courageous life. Here you will find one hundred and thirty of my favorite quotations from some of the world's greatest thinkers, looking at courage through many distinctive lenses—wise, funny, spiritual, philosophical, historic, artistic, religious, eccentric.

Poets are perennially drawn to the subject of courage because it touches us at our deepest core, speaking to the very essence of what it means to be alive—what poet Jack Gilbert calls "the evident conclusion of being." For this reason, limiting this book to include only thirty poems with courage as their central theme was one of the toughest challenges I faced.

I open this book with John O'Donohue's "For Courage," a poem that sets the stage for an exploration of how a new understanding of courage can illuminate our lives and change everything it touches. This wonderful poem shines a spotlight on the possibility of creating courage out of life's darkest sources, moments when the very notion of courage seems unfathomable.

I also offer thirteen stories of individuals whose courage defines them, each in a different way. These are chosen from among the hundreds I had the privilege of encountering—testament to the defining power of courage in so many lives.

Investigating the wonderful quality of generosity for my first book, *Inspiring Generosity*, taught me that we are all innately generous. If we are lucky, something, sometime, calls it forth, bringing into the light what I call "a lightning bolt of generosity." But the true lesson from that book for me was that, when we experience an unexpected burst of generosity, it quite often changes us forever, leaving us standing in a new place, in a new orientation, with little appetite for going back to our former life.

All the lessons of generosity are very much alive in this exploration of courage. As with generosity, what interests me most is not a single spontaneous act but rather a life that is lived in a new orientation. The person who runs into the burning building to save a child engages in an act of bravery that leaves us awestruck—but what were the seeds of that act, and how does that act then inform the rest of that person's life?

So often, it seems, the person running into that building does not feel that she is doing anything extraordinary. Time after time, we hear these heroes say, "There's nothing special about what I did. Anybody would have done it. I was just doing what was put in my path." But the single act can often be traced back through a series of seemingly ordinary, everyday choices that gradually accumulate into something much larger. And, after bringing the child out of that burning building, the compass of the rescuer's life often changes forever. From that act, a life in alignment with one's truest values unfolds,

REST NOT.

LIFE IS SWEEPING BY;

GO AND DARE

BEFORE YOU DIE.

SOMETHING MIGHTY AND SUBLIME

LEAVE BEHIND TO CONQUER TIME!

JOHANN WOLFGANG VON GOETHE

IF YOU BRING FORTH WHAT IS
WITHIN YOU, WHAT YOU BRING
FORTH WILL SAVE YOU.

IF YOU DO NOT BRING FORTH
WHAT IS WITHIN YOU,
WHAT YOU DO NOT BRING FORTH
WILL DESTROY YOU.

THE GOSPEL OF THOMAS

marked by commitment, authenticity, and a willingness to take on tremendous risk. As Pema Chödrön teaches, "Deep down in the human spirit, there is a reservoir of courage. It is always available, always waiting to be discovered."

I have always been drawn to courageous lives, to people who stand up to be counted, who speak truth to power, who take risks and feel joy in living boldly. Quite often, these bolder lives are not filled with flash and dazzle, but are instead of a quieter nature, marked by a humble determination to make the most of the gifts life gives us.

WHAT IS COURAGE?

Our first clue lies in the word's derivation, from the Latin *cor* (the root of *coeur* in French and *cuore* in Italian), meaning "heart." What is it to act from one's heart? To live from one's heart? This is not some soft, New Age metaphor for doing whatever we want, what pleases us most. I believe that the word's root reveals that, when we act courageously, we are responding to our deepest selves, often unknown until the moment of being tested—what O'Donohue describes as "a courageous hospitality towards what is difficult, painful and unknown."

Why is it then that the courageous act feels so utterly natural? Nothing is forced. It is a feeling of opening up to who we are most authentically, against all odds, and withstanding all risks. Who we are in that moment feels in perfect alignment with who we recognize our true self to be, and what defines us.

Many confuse courage with fearlessness, but the courageous are actually very intimate with fear and have moved through it to the other shore. In the words of Nelson Mandela, "I learned that courage was not the absence of fear, but the triumph over it. The brave man is not he who does not feel afraid, but he who conquers that fear."

WE CAN DO

NO GREAT THINGS.

ONLY SMALL THINGS WITH

GREAT LOVE.

OFTEN ATTRIBUTED TO
MOTHER TERESA

There is a strong element of faith in courage—faith in the truth of who we are and where that will lead us, faith in what we are doing and its importance and value in the lives of others.

Courage shows up in our lives in thousands of unexpected ways. Forgiving can be an act of courage. Reconciliation can take courage. Deciding not to fight can sometimes be as courageous as charging into battle. Activism and ferociously committing one's life to benefit others can tap into great courage. Standing up to bullies and terrorists requires courage, as does undergoing surgery and cancer treatments, and giving birth. Falling in love and creating art are both courageous in their own ways. Learning a new skill, starting a business, and athletic achievement can require determined courage. There is tremendous courage in comforting the dying, asking for help, and taking great risks for great causes. Living with compassion and an open heart can also require courage of a different stripe. In my own life, I'm learning the courage required by aging.

The defining core of courage is love. Without love, courage is not possible. Acts of bravado, yes—but true courage is the natural outgrowth of our love of all that we hold dear, of the preciousness of each human life and a deep belief that what we love matters. Without love, there is nothing at stake, nothing to fight for.

THE MANY FACES OF COURAGE

In selecting the thirteen stories for this book, I took a long and inspiring tour through the many ways that courage can define our lives. I am humbled by all the courageous lives I witnessed in researching this book, and bow deeply to all the hundreds that space would not allow me to include. I especially regret not telling the stories of heroes in our armed services and police and fire departments who put their lives on the line every day; those in medicine and all the healing professions; teachers; leaders in business and government; and brave activists on the front lines of the struggles for equality, peace, and justice and against the travesty of incarceration in our country and our seemingly insatiable need to be perpetually at war.

Why do all these examples of courageous lives speak to us so poignantly? I think it is because we are living through a time of profound longing for heroes, in a world marked by fear in the face of faceless power.

The stories I have selected in these pages may shed light on the more surprising faces of courage, the courage found in everyday lives. No one profiled here is world famous. None has won the Nobel Prize or become a household name. Yet all teach that what can seem quite ordinary is often extraordinary courage.

I share the story of Debi Jackson (page 104), whose courage was the greatest gift she could offer her three-year-old transgender daughter as they navigated largely uncharted territory together, with love and courage as their guides.

I have been touched by countless stories of the courage of the dying—those in war zones, those living with terminal illness. When life is on the line and death is closing in, this is when we often find the courage to live full out. As author Anne Lamott reminds us, "The worst thing you can do when you are down in the dumps, . . . is to take a walk with dying friends. They will ruin everything for you." I share the story of Jennifer Glass (page 68) whose courage enabled her activism for the rights of the dying as she faced her own terminal diagnosis.

We tend to think that enduring great pain and suffering is the truest mark of courage, but sometimes it is making the choice to walk away from pain that requires the greatest courage—leaving a relationship that has become impossible to repair or revive, a career that has lost its potency, or ideas and institutions that hold us back. As researcher and organizational consultant Margaret Wheatley reminds us so eloquently, it can define our lives when we "walk out to walk in." She offers a test question to ask ourselves periodically in this regard: "What might I need to walk out of?" Courage and determination have defined the life of Jean Clarke-Mitchell (page 167), first as a victim of an abusive marriage and now in devoting her professional life to helping women who are victims of sexual assault and violence.

When we are young, we are afforded the chance to try on courage in its many guises. We can push ourselves to our edge in sports or academics. We can stand up to bullies and speak up for the unpopular or afraid. We can imagine our futures lived boldly, and then take the first tentative steps along the path. When I was vice president of Bennington College, I was always inspired to hear the president greet the incoming freshmen, urging them to take the courses that frightened them, offering them the chance to practice courage. It is a joy to share the story of the remarkable Gaby Chavez Hernandez (page 184), whose courage defined her as a very young child and, at the age of twenty-two, has already led her into the future that she dared to dream.

In his twenties, college student Tim DeChristopher seized an unanticipated moment of courage that has set the course for a life devoted to extraordinarily bold commitment and activism (page 16). Opening to courage so powerfully made it impossible for him to live any less fully.

To be a journalist in our times requires having the courage to put oneself on the line every day. In our country, what used to be the peaceful beat of our Main Streets is now often charged with hatred and violence. And the reporters who go to remote war zones do so believing that the value of their contribution outweighs the heavy risks. The Newseum, an interactive museum of journalism in Washington, DC, lists the names of 2,200 journalists who have died reporting the news. In 2014 alone, fifty journalists were killed in the line of work, some cruelly and publicly beheaded. Three books have been especially revealing windows on this world for me: war photographer Lynsey Addario's *It's What I Do,* written after the author was captured in Libya in March 2011; *Zen Under Fire,* by Marianne Elliott, a human rights activist and photojournalist in the Middle East and Asia; and *The Lonely War: One Woman's Account of the Struggle for Modern Iran,* by Nazila Fathi, whose courageous life is the focus of the story on page 150.

In the space of a few hours, a fatal car accident tore apart professor of Italian literature and writer Joseph Luzzi's charmed life, leaving him a grieving widower and father of a newborn. For Joe, courage did not come easily. He forced himself to search for it everywhere, and ultimately was able to find it in a most unexpected and inspiring place.

The stories of Edith and Loet Velmans (page 35) poignantly demonstrate the ways in which early courageous experiences can plant the seeds that grow and flourish throughout long lives and, many years later, bloom into a final chapter of joy and gratitude for lives lived fully.

Diana Nyad (whose story appears on page 51) has been a hero to me for many decades because I, too, am a swimmer. But I've realized, in looking more deeply at her story, that her courage has nothing to do with her breathtaking feats in the water. The ocean is simply the setting in which her astonishing spiritual courage manifests.

For the remarkable Buddhist teacher Allan Lokos (page 89), who survived a catastrophic plane accident and a long series of surgeries and treatments that ultimately gave him back his life, courage was the essential element for recreating his shattered life.

I have felt for some time that a commitment to a life of disciplined spiritual practice requires great courage. Buddhist teacher Larry Yang (page 133) lived a young life marked by discrimination, addiction, and exclusion. Meditation practice helped him navigate the choppy waters of recovery, and ultimately opened a path of Buddhist study and practice, as well as a dedication to actively serving the underserved.

Congolese prosecutor Amani Mirielle Kahatwa (who is profiled on page 117) stands up to the strong and powerful every day as she seeks out and brings to justice those who have used rape as a weapon of war. Her courage serves as both the voice of, and the inspiration for, those too fearful to speak up.

MY OWN JOURNEY TO COURAGE

My childhood, like so many others, was marked by long periods of challenge and sadness. In comparison to the vast majority of the world's childhood traumas, those in my privileged life now seem very small indeed—but, at the time, they were quite overwhelming. When I look back, I realize that I always held the unshakable belief that I was headed into a life in which I would have some extra armor of resistance, determination, and strength. But not everyone is so fortunate.

In adulthood's toughest times, I could nearly always feel the strength of the earlier training ground. That strength grew to become an old friend: "Well, there you are again. Thanks for sticking around!" As I have faced other losses, sadness, and tragedies, I always had some mysterious reserve of something I could not yet name. I knew I was strong, determined, and compassionate, but never thought to use the word "courageous." After immersing myself in so many stories of courage, I now feel a kinship. Nothing more, nothing less.

A much beloved teacher and friend, Mu Soeng, offers this seemingly simple recipe for a life well lived: *Live simply, care deeply, die joyfully.* Simple, that is, if you add courage as the essential ingredient in the mix.

During the writing of this book, my son was diagnosed with cancer—the single most terrifying thing I could imagine. Now, having come through the storms of surgery and treatment, we all rejoice in his return to vibrant, good health, relishing our great good fortune and able to see the courage that carried us all through this journey. I always knew Charlie was courageous. Now he has become truly intimate with courage. This book belongs to Charlie and all those who search their hearts for the courage to face life's greatest challenges.

WE ARE ALL COURAGEOUS in our own ways—some of us have simply had it tested a bit more than others. Such trials are the stuff of life that we would never wish for but, at the end of the tunnel, find ourselves grateful for having passed through them. Like love, courage never goes away, only changes form from time to time, builds on itself, evolves, expands, and enhances everything it touches.

In offering you this book, my hope is that you will tap into the fire of your own inner courage and feel its transformative power to light your way.

FEAR IS THE CHEAPEST
ROOM IN THE HOUSE.
I WOULD LIKE TO SEE YOU LIVING IN
BETTER CONDITIONS.

HAFIZ

FOR COURAGE

When the light around you lessens
And your thoughts darken until
Your body feels fear turn
Cold as a stone inside

When you find yourself bereft
Of any belief in yourself
And all you unknowingly
Leaned on has fallen

When one voice commands
Your whole heart,
And it is raven dark,

Steady yourself and see
That it is your own thinking
That darkens your world

Search and you will find
A diamond-thought of light,

Know that you are not alone
And that this darkness has purpose
Gradually it will school your eyes
To find the one gift your life requires
Hidden within this night-corner.

Invoke the learning
Of every suffering
You have suffered.

Close your eyes
Gather all the kindling
About your heart
To create one spark.
That is all you need

To nourish the flame

That will cleanse the dark

Of its weight of festered fear.

A new confidence will come alive

To urge you towards higher ground

Where your imagination

Will learn to engage difficulty

As its most rewarding threshold!

JOHN O'DONOHUE

> ## "PRINCIPLED ACTION IS THE SALVATION OF THE SOUL."
>
> TIM DeCHRISTOPHER

Tim DeChristopher

WE OFTEN FAIL to appreciate the intensity of our own innate courage until the moment in which it is unmistakably called forth. For every person of great courage I have come to know in writing this book, that moment is one of profound clarity and recognition of their greatest authenticity, and an alignment with the values they hold most dear. For climate activist Tim DeChristopher who has become quite intimate with moments of great courage over recent years, these are what he calls "defining moments of self-identity," breakthroughs that bring forth the most genuine self.

Tim's journey to a courageous life seems rather straightforward in the telling—a listing of events and dates. But his life has been an evolution of experiences and qualities of character, each building on the earlier ones, until a defining moment of courage changed everything so there could be no turning back.

As a student at the University of Utah in 2007, Tim became increasingly immersed in and moved by his study of the climate crisis. While taking his final exams that December, he decided to join leading climate activists in protesting a controversial (later proven to be illegal) land auction, orchestrated by the Bush administration, that included parcels adjacent to the treasured Arches and Canyonlands National Parks. The principal bidders at the auction were oil and gas companies whose goal was to use the land for drilling.

After his last exam on December 19, Tim went to the auction in Salt Lake City to join the protest. To his astonishment, he was able to enter the auction room itself and register as a bidder. He was given a numbered paddle (later making him the famous "Bidder 70" of the film of that name) with which to place his bids on the land parcels. While his intention had been to make a speech or disrupt the proceedings in some way, he quickly saw an opportunity for greater impact. As parcel after parcel came up for bidding, he raised his paddle, at first simply driving up the prices and then placing winning bids of up to $1.2 million. When authorities realized his actions were in protest and not legitimate bids, the auction was shut down and Tim was taken into custody.

In speaking with me about what that moment of stepping forward felt like, Tim remembered clearly thinking, "This is really risky—and I have to do it anyway." Courage, he said, felt like "pushing through that internal dialogue" in a matter of minutes and doing what needed to be done.

During the two years it took the federal government to try, convict, and sentence Tim, his action that day galvanized a new energy not only in the climate movement but also in our understanding of civil disobedience. As founder and leader of the organization Peaceful Uprising, Tim toured the country urging boldness in speaking out and fighting for climate justice. As he continued to uncover his increasingly strong voice, the movement grew dramatically. Activists, organizers, and advocates from all over the country came to demonstrate solidarity at every phase of Tim's trial.

Tim was ultimately sentenced to two years in federal prison. At his sentencing, emboldened by the force of the movement he was now spearheading, he inspired his supporters with these words: "At this point of unimaginable threats on the horizon, this is what hope looks like. In these times of morally bankrupt government that has sold out its principles, this is what patriotism looks like. With countless lives on the line, this is what love looks like, and it will only grow."

Released from prison in April 2013, Tim attended Harvard Divinity School (a dean tells me this was a rare application made from prison), where he studied justice movements. In December 2015, he and I were able to spend time speaking about his courageous journey and about the role of courage in all our lives in this pivotal moment in human history.

As one might expect from a divinity student, Tim's manner is thoughtful and reflective, and he is deeply interested in probing the larger questions. At the same time, he seems perpetually poised for action. In considering what courageous lives look like, he emphasizes "the courage to be vulnerable—to break out from what we expect from one another." He singles out this quality of vulnerability as "a cornerstone of much of great activism." He continued, "When people see someone making themselves vulnerable, it is disorienting. That disorientation has the power to inspire and change. It creates interest in bringing real courage into our actions and disruption from the status quo. Courage is a practice, a muscle that can be built."

As founder and leader of the Climate Disobedience Center, Tim is passionate in his belief that the very civil disobedience that has shaped our country and our laws is what is required to meet today's climate crisis. It will always involve risk, he says. We need to be guided by what he calls an "unreasonable morality" that upholds values and principles even when doing so might not seem logical. A spiritually guided movement resists reasons to sell out and values truth above all else. "Movements with soul come out of hardship and suffering," Tim says. But, as he knows all too well, not everyone has an appetite for struggle. Never easily discouraged, he finds the greatest frustration in his work is "that cowardice and self-interest frame the world for so many that they don't even see it."

At the very heart of Tim's beliefs is the conviction that the greatest challenge facing us is a "spiritual struggle . . . a movement of the heart, not just the head . . . to be in alignment with our values and nurture innate courage." As Thoreau said, the task is "to bring conscience to bear." Tim underscores the role of faith in the civil disobedience he embraces. For him, the essential questions are these: *How do we hold onto our values? How do we maintain our humanity? How do we create communities of courage that feel part of the great web of existence?* As to his role in this movement: "My job now is to inspire people and teach courage."

All the individuals profiled in this book lead courageous lives. Tim stands out as one who embraces the courage at the center of his life as the source of what he hopes will be his greatest contribution. He is already a hero to so many at such a young age, and it is inspiring to consider the potential impact of his future life and work in a time that cries out for courageous and creative leadership.

THE MINUTE A PERSON WHOSE
WORD MEANS A GREAT DEAL
TO OTHERS **DARES** TO TAKE
THE OPEN-HEARTED AND
COURAGEOUS WAY,
MANY OTHERS FOLLOW.

MARIAN ANDERSON

MORALITY

MAY CONSIST SOLELY

IN THE COURAGE OF

MAKING A CHOICE.

LEON BLUM

THE SECRET IS TO LEAP

The secret is to leap
widely and strangely
over the deep,
not knowing
what's down there,
But pretty certain
in some crevice
there must be a small
purple flower.

DICK ALLEN

AND WHAT HE GREATLY

THOUGHT,

HE NOBLY

DARED.

HOMER

MANIFESTO:
THE MAD FARMER LIBERATION FRONT

Love the quick profit, the annual raise,
vacation with pay. Want more
of everything ready-made. Be afraid
to know your neighbors and to die.
And you will have a window in your head.
Not even your future will be a mystery
any more. Your mind will be punched
   in a card
and shut away in a little drawer.
When they want you to buy something
they will call you. When they want you
to die for profit they will let you know.
So, friends, every day do something
that won't compute. Love the Lord.
Love the world. Work for nothing.
Take all that you have and be poor.
Love someone who does not deserve it.
Denounce the government and embrace

the flag. Hope to live in that free
republic for which it stands.
Give your approval to all you cannot
understand. Praise ignorance, for what man
has not encountered he has not destroyed.
Ask the questions that have no answers.
Invest in the millennium. Plant sequoias.
Say that your main crop is the forest
that you did not plant,
that you will not live to harvest.
Say that the leaves are harvested
when they have rotted into the mold.
Call that profit. Prophesy such returns.
Put your faith in the two inches of humus
that will build under the trees
every thousand years. Listen to carrion—
   put your ear
close, and hear the faint chattering

of the songs that are to come.
Expect the end of the world. Laugh.
Laughter is immeasurable. Be joyful
though you have considered all the facts.
So long as women do not go cheap
for power, please women more than men.
Ask yourself: Will this satisfy
a woman satisfied to bear a child?
Will this disturb the sleep
of a woman near to giving birth?
Go with your love to the fields.
Lie down in the shade. Rest your head
in her lap. Swear allegiance
to what is nighest your thoughts.
As soon as the generals and the politicos
can predict the motions of your mind,
lose it. Leave it as a sign

to mark the false trail, the way
you didn't go.
Be like the fox
who makes more tracks than necessary,
some in the wrong direction.
Practice resurrection.

WENDELL BERRY

DON'T BEND;

DON'T WATER IT DOWN;

DON'T TRY TO MAKE IT

LOGICAL;

DON'T EDIT YOUR OWN SOUL

ACCORDING TO THE FASHION.

RATHER, FOLLOW YOUR MOST

INTENSE OBSESSIONS

MERCILESSLY. FRANZ KAFKA

THERE COMES A TIME

WHEN ONE MUST TAKE A POSITION

THAT IS NEITHER SAFE,

NOR POLITIC, NOR POPULAR,

BUT HE MUST TAKE IT

BECAUSE CONSCIENCE TELLS HIM

IT IS RIGHT.

MARTIN LUTHER KING, JR.

A MAN OF COURAGE
NEVER NEEDS WEAPONS,
BUT HE MAY NEED BAIL.

LEWIS MUMFORD

LET US GO FORTH
WITH FEAR AND COURAGE
AND RAGE
TO SAVE THE WORLD.

GRACE PALEY

CLOUDY DAY

It is windy today. A wall of wind crashes against,
windows clunk against, iron frames
as wind swings past broken glass
and seethes, like a frightened cat
in empty spaces of the cellblock.

In the exercise yard
we sat huddled in our prison jackets,
on our haunches against the fence,
and the wind carried our words
over the fences,
while the vigilant guard on the tower
held his cap at the sudden gust.

I could see the main tower from where I sat,
and the wind in my face
gave me the feeling I could grasp
the tower like a cornstalk,
and snap it from its roots of rock.

The wind plays it like a flute,
this hollow shoot of rock.
The brim girded with barbwire
with a guard sitting there also,
listening intently to the sounds
as clouds cover the sun.

I thought of the day I was coming
    to prison,
in the back seat of a police car,
hands and ankles chained, the policeman
    pointed,
    "See that big water tank? The big
    silver one out there, sticking up?
    That's the prison."

And here I am, I cannot believe it.
Sometimes it is such a dream, a dream,
where I stand up in the face of the wind,
like now, it blows at my jacket,
and my eyelids flick a little bit,
while I stare disbelieving. . . .

The third day of spring,
and four years later, I can tell you,
how a man can endure, how a man
can become so cruel, how he can die
or become so cold. I can tell you this,
I have seen it every day, every day,
and still I am strong enough to love you,
love myself and feel good;
even as the earth shakes and trembles,
and I have not a thing to my name,
I feel as if I have everything, everything.

JIMMY SANTIAGO BACA

INDIVIDUAL COURAGE
IS THE ONLY INTERESTING THING
IN LIFE.

SIMONE SIGNORET

IT IS CURIOUS THAT
PHYSICAL COURAGE
SHOULD BE SO COMMON
IN THE WORLD,
AND MORAL COURAGE
SO RARE.

MARK TWAIN

FOLLOW THE PATH OF THE UNSAFE

INDEPENDENT THINKER.

EXPOSE YOUR IDEAS TO THE

DANGER of CONTROVERSY.

SPEAK YOUR MIND

AND FEAR LESS THE LABEL OF

"CRACKPOT"

THAN THE STIGMA OF CONFORMITY.

THOMAS J. WATSON

> "LET EVERYTHING HAPPEN TO YOU,
> BEAUTY AND TERROR
> JUST KEEP GOING.
> NO FEELING IS FINAL."
>
> RAINER MARIA RILKE

Edith and Loet Velmans

ONE OF THE most surprising effects of courageously enduring extraordinarily difficult times can sometimes be an utter lack of bitterness. In fact, courage itself can place a protective shield over the painful experience and bring inspiration and optimistic passion for a new future. Over and over, I have met courageous people and read their stories of surviving horrendous catastrophes and emerging from them with a passionate sense of optimism for a new beginning in a life unblemished by bitterness.

Edith and Loet Velmans are survivors of World War II who share both memories of harrowing experiences and a long and happy life together since the war's end. Each has a very different story. But now, sitting with my remarkable friends and listening to them tell the stories of their lives is to witness this complete lack of bitterness that has allowed their lives to unfold emboldened, rather than devastated by, the original tragic experience. And, like all the subjects of this book, the Velmans do not consider themselves unusually courageous. They see their stories as just two of many millions of survivors' journeys.

A young Jewish girl living a carefree childhood in the Netherlands when the Nazis invaded her country, Edith was taken in and protected by a Protestant family for the three years of Nazi occupation, "hiding in plain sight." She was more fortunate than most, including her compatriot Anne Frank, who went into hiding the same day as Edith. In order to avoid suspicion, Edith's new family even assigned her to look after a German officer billeted with them during the war, living in the room next to hers. While Edith does not name the courage in this experience, it is not difficult to see it as a central player.

At the beginning of the war, there were 140,000 Jews in the Netherlands. Fewer than 30,000 survived. Of those who were hidden, a third were discovered and murdered. Edith witnessed many of the war's horrors firsthand; her youth was completely eradicated; her country was decimated. She lost her mother, grandmother, brother, and countless friends in the Nazi camps. The scope of the tragedy was so vast that she describes her own experience as "commonplace"—adding "Everyone has their own burden." She emerged from those years in hiding and fear with grace, humor, and a determination to live a life of meaning. She attributes her strength and resilience to others and claims she did not show any unusual degree of courage in what she endured. To know Edith, however, is to see her history through a different lens.

What is the legacy of her courageous early journey? In a letter to a friend after the war, Edith summarizes the belief it kindled in her: "I believe in goodness, above all. And the beauty of life, the beauty in people . . . In all of us simmers something we had when we came into this world. Something good, something warm, something to do with love." These remarkable sentiments can only come from a spirit that was uncrushed by the tragedy she endured. While she always thought she would study to be a writer, her war experience led her to become a psychologist in order to help others. "I would not allow myself to be sad. It was a new world, and I knew what was required of me . . . to make the best of things, to turn over a new leaf."

Many years later, Edith brought Tine zur Kleinsmiede, the woman who hid her during the war, to Israel to be honored by Yad Vashem, the memorial to the victims of the Holocaust. In her speech at the ceremony, Tine echoed the refrain of so many other courageous heroes: "Anyone would have done the same thing, in my place."

Now ninety, Edith looks back on a life well lived, bravely embracing her own advanced years as a blessing, not focusing on diminutions but instead rejoicing in gifts. And the gift she gives us all is her best-selling memoir *Edith's Story: The True Story of a Young Girl's Courage, Love and Survival During WWII.*

As I listen to Loet describe his war years, I am struck by the sheer magnitude of his horrific experience and am left awed by the resilience of the human spirit. In May of 1940, as the Nazis moved into the Netherlands and Edith was being whisked into hiding, seventeen-year-old Loet was one of the last to escape, commandeering a small lifeboat with a capacity for four passengers—but that day miraculously holding forty-four other determined souls. His account of acquiring the boat in the chaos of the moment, organizing the passengers, locating his family and bringing them along, and plunging out across the North Sea to England against incalculable odds, is a story of single-minded, focused bravery—he did what needed to be done, immediately, for the benefit of others, with no second thoughts. He had a clear conviction and the determination to see it through. As we spoke, Loet was preparing to travel to Holland for a seventy-fifth-anniversary celebration of the perilous escape, attended by (among others) the only other living survivor of the voyage, as well as scores of descendants of family members of those who escaped with them.

After landing in England, Loet and his family moved to the Dutch East Indies in order to be farther from danger. As he says, "I became a fugitive, an escape artist, always one step ahead . . ." Then, on the island of Java in 1942, Loet was taken prisoner by the Japanese. What followed was imprisonment in Changi prison in Singapore, built for 600 but holding 10,000, and then three and a half years as a slave laborer and prisoner of war of the Japanese, who were building the infamous "Railway of Death" along the River Kwai on the Burma-Thailand border. During these years, Loet was continuously beaten, tortured, and starved, and suffered from malaria, dysentery, and a host of other maladies. More than 200,000 prisoners of war died during the march.

What was it that allowed Loet not only to survive but also to go on to lead a life of great good fortune? When I asked him about the experience, he described the valor of others, the lucky breaks, and his resilience and determination, but shied away from any use of the word "courage." Listening to Loet's protest made me realize that our cultural understanding of the word "courage" is far too narrow. For him, it was exactly his determination and resilience that *were* his courage. He kept going. He bounced back. He always held out for the future at the other end of the horror. Courage was, quite simply, never giving up.

At ninety-two, he looks back on what he calls a very "lucky" life, shaped to some degree by those horrific years. He sees those experiences as the root of his ability to take chances and make things happen as a leader in the world of business as chairman of the international public relations firm Hill & Knowlton. As he says, living through the worst that could happen released him from fear and gave him the freedom and boldness to embrace life wholeheartedly.

The Velmans' stories recall a distant history that is still palpably present to those who lived through it. Their full and rich lives together, their devotion to family, and their selfless service to others so clearly evolved from the early calls to courage that defined them seventy years ago—and that continue to define them as they live out their lives' final chapters.

NOTHING SPLENDID
HAS EVER BEEN ACHIEVED
EXCEPT BY THOSE WHO
DARED BELIEVE
THAT SOMETHING INSIDE THEM
WAS SUPERIOR
TO CIRCUMSTANCE.

BRUCE BARTON

COURAGE

IS WHAT IT TAKES

TO STAND UP AND SPEAK;

COURAGE IS ALSO WHAT IT TAKES TO

SIT DOWN AND LISTEN.

WINSTON CHURCHILL

IF WE DID THE THINGS

WE ARE CAPABLE OF,

WE WOULD LITERALLY

ASTOUND OURSELVES.

THOMAS A. EDISON

THE BEST WAY OUT
IS ALWAYS THROUGH.

ROBERT FROST

MOTHER TO SON

Well, son, I'll tell you:

Life for me ain't been no crystal stair.

It's had tacks in it,
And splinters,

And boards torn up,

And places with no carpet on
the floor—

Bare.

But all the time

I'se been a-climbin' on,

And reachin' landin's,

And turnin' corners,

And sometimes goin' in the dark

Where there ain't been no light.

So, boy, don't you turn back.

Don't you set down on the steps.

'Cause you finds it's kinder hard.

Don't you fall now—

For I'se still goin', honey,

I'se still climbin',

And life for me ain't been no
crystal stair.

LANGSTON HUGHES

COURAGE IS CONTAGIOUS.
WHEN A BRAVE MAN
TAKES A STAND,
THE SPINES OF OTHERS
ARE OFTEN STIFFENED.

BILLY GRAHAM

IF

If you can keep your head when all about you
    Are losing theirs and blaming it on you,
If you can trust yourself when all men doubt you,
    But make allowance for their doubting too;
If you can wait and not be tired by waiting,
    Or being lied about, don't deal in lies,
Or being hated, don't give way to hating,
    And yet don't look too good, nor talk too wise:

If you can dream—and not make dreams your master;
    If you can think—and not make thoughts your aim;
If you can meet with Triumph and Disaster
    And treat those two impostors just the same;
If you can bear to hear the truth you've spoken
    Twisted by knaves to make a trap for fools,
Or watch the things you gave your life to, broken,
    And stoop and build 'em up with worn-out tools:

If you can make one heap of all your winnings
  And risk it on one turn of pitch-and-toss,
And lose, and start again at your beginnings
  And never breathe a word about your loss;
If you can force your heart and nerve and sinew
  To serve your turn long after they are gone,
And so hold on when there is nothing in you
  Except the Will which says to them: 'Hold on!'

If you can talk with crowds and keep your virtue,
  Or walk with Kings—nor lose the common touch,
If neither foes nor loving friends can hurt you,
  If all men count with you, but none too much;
If you can fill the unforgiving minute
  With sixty seconds' worth of distance run,
Yours is the Earth and everything that's in it,
  And—which is more—you'll be a Man, my son!

RUDYARD KIPLING

ONE MAN WITH COURAGE IS A MAJORITY.

THOMAS JEFFERSON

WE NEED THE COURAGE TO LEARN FROM OUR PAST AND NOT LIVE IN IT.

SHARON SALZBERG

KEEP YOUR FEARS TO YOURSELF, BUT SHARE YOUR COURAGE WITH OTHERS.

ROBERT LOUIS STEVENSON

"I'VE MISSED MORE THAN NINE THOUSAND SHOTS IN
MY CAREER. I'VE LOST ALMOST THREE HUNDRED GAMES.
TWENTY-SIX TIMES I'VE BEEN TRUSTED TO TAKE
THE GAME-WINNING SHOT AND MISSED. I'VE FAILED
OVER AND OVER AND OVER AGAIN IN MY LIFE.
AND THAT IS WHY I SUCCEED."

MICHAEL JORDAN

Diana Nyad

GREAT ACCOMPLISHMENTS by champion athletes have always struck me as breath-taking lessons in determination, endurance, and will. But occasionally an athlete reaches into the stratosphere for an achievement that can only have come about through the greatest courage. In the realm of courageous physical achievement, Diana Nyad is in a class by herself.

As a child growing up in Florida, Diana knew the ocean was her realm when she stood on the beach for the first time. Swimming at age one, competing by age ten, breaking records throughout her teenage years, she always wanted to be in the water. A world champion by the time she hit her twenties, Diana first came into public awareness with her record-breaking swim around Manhattan in 1975.

With such a record of achievement, her dream of swimming from Cuba to Florida seemed within reach. But, in 1978, at the age of twenty-eight, she was forced to abandon that goal halfway through her first attempt in those treacherous waters. Not wanting to end her swimming career with this dashed attempt, at thirty she broke the distance record by swimming nonstop the 102 miles from Bimini in the Bahamas to Juno Beach, Florida. She then stayed out of the water for the next three decades.

At the age of sixty, a few months after her mother's death, Diana felt her own mortality closing in and the long-dormant dream of the Cuba-to-Florida swim resurfaced. While it had seemed out of reach in all the intervening years, it had never gone away. As she said, "This dream lived somewhere in my imagination for thirty years from the first spark of magic lit when I was in my twenties." She got back in the pool to see what was possible.

Swimming any tough competition at that age, not having trained for over thirty years, would be an uphill battle—and to tackle the very toughest challenge in ocean swimming seemed folly. As she assessed her chances of success, Diana says she knew it would all boil down to "emotional courage." One can retrain muscles, push endurance to the limit, and exert superhuman will and determination. But the X-factor is courage.

That initial swim led to years of ferocious training—from twenty laps on the first day to eight-hour ocean swims, then ten and twelve, fifteen and eighteen, in the Caribbean and Mexico. With single-minded focus, Diana got herself into the best shape of her life and jumped into the Cuban waters once again in 2010, so many years after her first attempts. And, once again, fate was not on her side. Nor was it during her subsequent tries in 2011 and in 2012, when she nearly lost her life to her most dangerous ocean enemy, the box jellyfish, which emits an often fatal poison. She was in shark-infested waters and often in rough water. After her second try, Diana owned up to having been uncharacteristically devastated—for about twenty-four hours. "But at the thirty-hour mark, I felt the surge of the mettle within."

By 2012, she had assembled a remarkable team of trainers, navigators, and shark and jellyfish teams, and had researched every contingency from every direction. But, after four attempts, the team said no more. Nearly everyone tried to talk her out of one last try at age sixty-four. Diana forged ahead, quoting Thomas Edison: "Our greatest weakness is giving up. The most certain way to success is to try one more time."

Looking back over a life that led her to this final swim, Diana sees the spirit that brought her there. "At two, three, four, I believe I heard some version of 'Reveille' in my spirit, at the crack of dawn, and went to bed exhausted at the end of each day, having put out so much that there wasn't a fingernail more to give." In every challenge she has faced, she has always given the ultimate credit to "the power of the human spirit."

If she were to be successful, the Cuba-to-Florida swim would break records and achieve what many had called impossible. But, for Diana, "this swim was about reawakening to a bold life, a calling to fill my days with acute passion, goals more noble than actually making it from Cuba to Florida. I refuse to take a place among timid souls."

On September 2, 2013, at the age of sixty-four, after thirty-five years and four failures, Diana Nyad walked out of the water and onto the beach in Key West after swimming 111 miles in 53 hours, the first person to achieve this milestone without a shark cage to protect her. Addressing the cheering crowd, she acknowledged that what she had just achieved was never really about swimming. Her message was to never give up and to believe that dreams can be achieved regardless of age. Like all the truly courageous, she had acted utterly in alignment with her most closely held values, and had done so while serving as a loving inspiration for those who heard her message. In her words, she had been guided by "utter conviction and unwavering passion and the ultimate dream."

NOAH WAS A BRAVE MAN
TO SAIL IN A WOODEN BOAT
WITH TWO TERMITES.

ANONYMOUS

COURAGE AND PERSEVERANCE HAVE A MAGICAL TALISMAN, BEFORE WHICH DIFFICULTIES DISAPPEAR AND OBSTACLES VANISH INTO AIR.

JOHN QUINCY ADAMS

COURAGE
IS GOING FROM
FAILURE TO FAILURE
WITHOUT LOSING
ENTHUSIASM.

OFTEN ATTRIBUTED TO
WINSTON CHURCHILL

SWEET DARKNESS

When your eyes are tired
the world is tired also.

When your vision has gone
no part of the world can find you.

Time to go into the dark
where the night has eyes
to recognize its own.

There you can be sure
you are not beyond love.

The dark will be your womb
tonight.

The night will give you a horizon
further than you can see.

You must learn one thing.
The world was made to be free in

Give up all the other worlds
except the one to which you belong.

Sometimes it takes darkness and
    the sweet

confinement of your aloneness
to learn

anything or anyone
that does not bring you alive

is too small for you.

DAVID WHYTE

ONLY THOSE WHO WILL
RISK GOING TOO FAR
CAN POSSIBLY FIND OUT
HOW FAR
ONE CAN GO.

T. S. ELIOT

MAN CANNOT
DISCOVER NEW OCEANS
UNLESS HE HAS
THE COURAGE TO LOSE SIGHT OF
THE SHORE.

ANDRÉ GIDE

ONCE MORE MY NOW BEWILDERED DOVE

Once more, my now bewildered Dove
Bestirs her puzzled wings.
Once more, her mistress, on the deep
Her troubled question flings—

Thrice to the floating casement
The Patriarch's bird returned—
Courage! My brave Columba!
There may yet be *Land!*

EMILY DICKINSON

THE GREATEST TEST
OF COURAGE ON EARTH
IS TO BEAR DEFEAT
WITHOUT LOSING HEART.

ROBERT GREEN INGERSOLL

THERE IS NOTHING
IN THE WORLD
SO MUCH ADMIRED
AS A MAN WHO KNOWS
HOW TO BEAR
UNHAPPINESS
WITH COURAGE.

SENECA

A SHIP IN HARBOR IS SAFE, BUT THAT IS NOT WHAT SHIPS ARE BUILT FOR.

JOHN SHEDD

INVICTUS

Out of the night that covers me,
    Black as the pit from pole to pole,
I thank whatever gods may be
    For my unconquerable soul.

In the fell clutch of circumstance
    I have not winced nor cried aloud.
Under the bludgeonings of chance
    My head is bloody, but unbowed.

Beyond this place of wrath and tears
    Looms but the Horror of the shade,
And yet the menace of the years
    Finds and shall find me unafraid.

It matters not how strait the gate,
    How charged with punishments the scroll,
I am the master of my fate,
    I am the captain of my soul.

WILLIAM ERNEST HENLEY

THERE ARE ONLY

TWO MISTAKES

ONE CAN MAKE

ALONG THE ROAD TO TRUTH:

NOT GOING

ALL THE WAY, AND

NOT STARTING.

ANONYMOUS

I'VE BEEN THROUGH IT ALL, BABY.

I'M MOTHER
COURAGE.

ELIZABETH TAYLOR

> "LET US NOT PRAY TO BE SHELTERED FROM DANGERS
> BUT TO BE FEARLESS WHEN FACING THEM."
>
> RABINDRANATH TAGORE

Jennifer Glass

WE ALL WONDER what we would do if faced with a sudden, terminal diagnosis and, of course, none of us knows the answer with any certainty at all. Would we spend our life savings on a trip around the world, or crawl into a ball and tune life out in our sorrow? Would we share our news or keep it to ourselves? And what would be our spiritual path to understanding that death is on the near horizon? The lucky among us will access our innate courage in order to focus on giving the end of life as much meaning and dignity as possible. For some, the journey is easier than for others.

There was nothing remotely easy about Jennifer Glass's journey. Nonetheless, she drew upon the ferocious, unflinching courage to make a long-lasting impact—not only for herself but also for all those faced with one of life's greatest challenges.

Married just four months and celebrating Christmas with her husband, stepchildren, family, and friends in her newly renovated home, Jennifer, a successful communications executive, seemed to have everything. As her husband, Harlan, lovingly massaged her neck one evening during the holiday, he felt several hard, pea-sized lumps that distressed him. Several weeks later, the lumps were diagnosed as cancerous lymph nodes that had metastasized from an aggressive and inoperable stage 3B lung cancer. Given the type of cancer and its stage of progression, Jennifer's chances of surviving five years were no more than five percent. As she later said, she and Harlan had never anticipated that the phrase "in sickness and in health" would be put to the test quite so quickly.

Having relished the life of an adventurer—backpacking through South America, teaching in Asia, and successfully climbing the corporate ladders at Oracle, Intuit, Sony, and Facebook—Jennifer immediately committed to the most aggressive radiation and chemotherapy treatments available to tackle her particular cancer. After many months, she entered remission, as the tumors disappeared from her neck and the growth of those in her lung appeared to have been halted. Throughout the ordeal, her attitude was one of fighting the disease with everything she could summon, while, at the same time, making peace with death on an ever-encroaching horizon. When asked what guided her, she responded, "I'm not fearless, of course. But I have found ways to fear less."

Wanting to help others facing similar fates, Jennifer put her well-honed communications skills to work in forcefully speaking out, with stories on the Huffington Post; a video that she and Harlan produced, "A Photo a Day: One Year with Cancer"; motivational speaking engagements; and active appeals to the California legislature to enact end-of-life options for the dying. As she said over and over, "I have cancer, and I want to die on my own terms."

Jennifer was inspired by the example of twenty-nine-year-old Brittany Maynard, whose story was covered extensively by the press when she moved from California (where Jennifer also lived) to Portland, Oregon, where aid in dying is legal. Brittany was suffering from terminal brain cancer and wanted to die peacefully and painlessly at her own hands. Wanting that option to be available for herself and others, Jennifer devoted the end of her life to boldly advocating for rights for the dying in her own state. "I believe I should have the legal choice to end my life calmly, peacefully, and with dignity," she said. "I want that for myself and I want that for the people I love. Everyone should have that choice."

Studies show that seven out of ten Americans support physician-assisted suicide for patients at the end of life with a terminal diagnosis. But only two states offer such legal options. As California debated this issue, Jennifer used her dwindling energy to lobby for a new law.

By June 2015, her cancer had become resistant to all chemotherapy drugs and had spread to the other lung and to her liver, abdomen, pelvis, cervix, and brain. And still she spoke out. Barely able to navigate the stairs at home, she somehow found the courage to navigate the halls of the state legislature to deliver her message: "I'm doing everything I can to extend my life. And I believe no one should have the right to prolong my death."

On August 6, 2015, a little more than a year and a half after her diagnosis, Jennifer entered a palliative coma in which she no longer took food or water. She died five days later, with her family beside her. While she had not won the battle to control her death as she wanted, she died knowing that she had used all the courage she could summon to face the end of her life with a strong and bold voice, determined to make a difference for others who would follow.

COURAGE IS FEAR THAT HAS SAID ITS PRAYERS.

KARLE WILSON BAKER

"Buddhist practices offer a way of saying 'Hey, come back over here, reconnect.' The only way that you'll actually wake up and have some freedom is if you have the capacity and courage to stay with the vulnerability and the discomfort."

TARA BRACH

FACING IT,
ALWAYS FACING IT,
THAT'S THE WAY TO GET THROUGH.
FACE IT.

JOSEPH CONRAD

"To live fully and willingly in the world

of the living is more brave even than going open-eyed toward

death. All too often we do neither, and, clinging to some

safer middle ground, end by feeling neither our terrors

nor our joys."

JANE HIRSHFIELD

FOR A FRIEND,
ON THE ARRIVAL OF ILLNESS

Now is the time of dark invitation
Beyond a frontier you did not expect;
Abruptly, your old life seems distant.

You barely noticed how each day opened
A path through fields never questioned,
Yet expected deep down to hold treasure.
Now your time on earth becomes full of threat;
Before your eyes your future shrinks.

You lived absorbed in the day to day,
So continuous with everything around you,
That you could forget you were separate;

Now this dark companion has come between you,
Distances have opened in your eyes,

You feel that against your will
A stranger has married your heart.

Nothing before has made you
Feel so isolated and lost.

When the reverberations of shock subside in you,
May grace come to restore you to balance.
May it shape a new space in your heart
To embrace this illness as a teacher
Who has come to open your life to new worlds.

May you find in yourself
A courageous hospitality
Towards what is difficult,
Painful and unknown.

May you use this illness
As a lantern to illuminate
The new qualities that will emerge in you.

May the fragile harvesting of this slow light

Help you to release whatever has become false in you.

May you trust this light to clear a path

Through all the fog of old unease and anxiety

Until you feel arising within you a tranquility

Profound enough to call the storm to stillness.

May you find the wisdom to listen to your illness:

Ask it why it came? Why it chose your friendship?

Where it wants to take you? What it wants you to know?

What quality of space it wants to create in you?

What you need to learn to become more fully yourself

That your presence may shine in the world.

May you keep faith with your body,

Learning to see it as a holy sanctuary

Which can bring this night-wound gradually

Towards the healing and freedom of dawn.

May you be granted the courage and vision

To work through passivity and self-pity,

To see the beauty you can harvest
From the riches of this dark invitation.

May you learn to receive it graciously,
And promise to learn swiftly
That it may leave you newborn,
Willing to dedicate your time to birth.

JOHN O'DONOHUE

"Courage is not simply one of the virtues,

but the form of every virtue at the testing point, which means at the

point of highest reality a chastity or honesty or mercy which yields

to danger will be chaste or honest or merciful only on conditions."

C. S. LEWIS

OUR DEEPEST FEARS
ARE LIKE DRAGONS
GUARDING OUR
DEEPEST TREASURE.

RAINER MARIA RILKE

COURAGE

IS THE CAPACITY

TO CONFRONT

WHAT CAN BE

IMAGINED.

LEO ROSTEN

VALOR
GROWS BY DARING,
FEAR BY HOLDING BACK.

PUBLILIUS SYRUS

THE OLD STOIC

Riches I hold in light esteem,
    And Love I laugh to scorn;
And lust of fame was but a dream,
    That vanished with the morn:

And if I pray, the only prayer
    That moves my lips for me
Is, "Leave the heart that now I bear,
    And give me liberty!"

Yes, as my swift days near their goal:
    'Tis all that I implore;
In life and death a chainless soul,
    With courage to endure.

EMILY BRONTË

I WENT TO THE WOODS BECAUSE
I WISHED TO LIVE DELIBERATELY,
TO FRONT ONLY THE ESSENTIAL
FACTS OF LIFE, AND SEE IF I COULD
NOT LEARN WHAT IT HAD TO TEACH,
AND NOT, WHEN I CAME TO DIE,
DISCOVER THAT I HAD NOT LIVED.

HENRY DAVID THOREAU

SUCCESS IS NEVER FINAL,
FAILURE IS NEVER FATAL.
IT'S COURAGE THAT COUNTS.

ANONYMOUS,
VARIOUSLY ATTRIBUTED

"And who is the person who, subject to death,
is not afraid or in terror of death? There is the case of the person who has abandoned passion, desire, fondness, thirst, fever, and craving for sensuality. Then he comes down with a serious disease. As he comes down with a serious disease, the thought does not occur to him, 'O, those beloved sensual pleasures will be taken from me, and I will be taken from them!' He does not grieve, is not tormented; does not weep, beat his breast, or grow delirious. This is a person who, subject to death, is not afraid or in terror of death."   THE BUDDHA

WHAT THE LIVING DO

Johnny, the kitchen sink has been clogged for days, some utensil probably
   fell down there.
And the Drano won't work but smells dangerous, and the crusty dishes
   have piled up

waiting for the plumber I still haven't called. This is the everyday we
   spoke of.
It's winter again: the sky's a deep, headstrong blue, and the sunlight
   pours through

the open living-room windows because the heat's on too high in here and
   I can't turn it off.
For weeks now, driving, or dropping a bag of groceries in the street,
   the bag breaking,

I've been thinking: This is what the living do. And yesterday, hurrying
   along those
wobbly bricks in the Cambridge sidewalk, spilling my coffee down my
   wrist and sleeve,

I thought it again, and again later, when buying a hairbrush: This is it.
Parking. Slamming the car door shut in the cold. What you called
that yearning.

What you finally gave up. We want the spring to come and the winter to
     pass. We want
whoever to call or not call, a letter, a kiss—we want more and more and
     then more of it.

But there are moments, walking, when I catch a glimpse of myself in the
     window glass,
say, the window of the corner video store, and I'm gripped by a cherishing
     so deep

for my own blowing hair, chapped face, and unbuttoned coat that I'm
     speechless:
I am living. I remember you.

MARIE HOWE

> "WE MUST LET GO OF THE LIFE WE'VE PLANNED
> SO AS TO HAVE THE LIFE THAT IS WAITING FOR US."
>
> JOSEPH CAMPBELL

Allan Lokos

WHEN WE READ accounts of catastrophes in which only a lucky few survive, we can't help but wonder how we could summon up the courage to escape death in a seemingly impossible situation, and then embark on a long and arduous path to healing and recovery. As Allan's story shows us, catastrophe can be the defining test of our lives—how we react in the moment and how we discover deep within ourselves the determination to not only endure but to endure well. It is a test that ultimately shifts the compass of our lives.

On Christmas Day of 2012, Buddhist teacher Allan Lokos and his wife Susanna were enjoying a long-awaited holiday in Burma. They were headed to Inle Lake, in Burma's Nyaungshwe Township, when their plane, with sixty-nine other passengers on board, crashed a mile short of the airport. As the plane filled with smoke and fire, passengers frantically searched for escape routes. Allan and Susanna found their way to an exit door, and Susanna was able to jump to the ground. Attempting to follow her, Allan got his foot stuck in part of the plane's floor. As he struggled to free himself, the fire caught up with him, and his body was completely engulfed in flames.

With an effort that can only be described as superhuman, Allan managed to extricate his foot and jump out of the burning plane. The fact that he survived these moments defies credulity. The fact that he also survived the journey through multiple surgeries, burn treatments, and all manner of therapies, first in Asia and later at home in New York, is equally miraculous. More than one doctor told Susanna that he wouldn't survive. Looking back, Allan says: "Even if a doctor had told me I wasn't going to make it, I wouldn't have accepted it." Allan's great strength and determination were what got him out of the plane and through the long years of recovery that followed. As he said to me as he looked back on that time, "I will own up to being very determined."

I first met Allan in June 2014, when we were both speakers at Buddhafest in Washington, DC. A much-beloved teacher and accomplished speaker, with a deep, resonant voice, Allan had just begun to speak publicly about what had happened to him. Believing that his experience of the last year and a half held lessons for us all, he had recently completed his moving memoir, *Through the Flames*. Still recovering from his ordeal, he spoke eloquently and with humor about the human capacity for facing seemingly unimaginable crises, pain, and disaster with strength and resolve.

Nearly a year later, some months after the book's publication, Allan and I sat down in his New York City living room to talk about the role of courage in his journey, and in all our journeys through life's most difficult moments. I was hesitant to ask him to relive the moments of the crash. But Allan took the lead and plunged in, describing, as he does in the book, the details of what had happened to him in those harrowing moments and in the months that followed. His account was moving beyond words, especially in its complete lack of bitterness and anger. Reliving the moments before escaping the plane, he described his emotional reaction as one of simultaneous terror and calm: "I was aware of the danger and still remained calm. I don't think one can conjure up that calmness without having the underpinnings that create it."

When I asked him about the role of courage in his ordeal and survival, he applied it not to himself but rather to Susanna, to his many doctors in Asia and New York, and to the army of helpers and generous friends who saw him through the ordeal. "There were times that were extremely difficult physically, mentally, and emotionally, during the healing process. During those times, effort and determination were necessary to survive. That requires reaching down to consciously summon one's resources. For me, those resources were developed during the many hours of mindful practice."

But the greatest test of Allan's determination was in his return home after many months in the hospital. Finally back in his own home after this long ordeal, he fell into a painful depression as he realized that he could not have his old life back. Everything had changed. Physically, mentally, and spiritually, he was evolving into a new person, and he knew he had to once again summon courage, this time to re-enter the world in a different way. "For me, courage was going back into the world."

Over the years, Allan had often taught the maxim, "Live life as the person you want to be." Now he had the chance to fully embody his teaching. The life he was living was not the life he thought he had signed on for. Or was it? As a Buddhist teacher, he discovered that all he held dear was being tested—and was also there to sustain him. Everything in his life had changed and was going to continue to change. The future was uncertain. His greatest challenge was accepting a changed life with understanding and the same determination that had seen him through his accident and recovery. In his words, "For many years, I have tried to integrate my meditation practice into my everyday life. The fact that I was calm and at peace most of the time allowed me to heal without unnecessary stress in an already stressful situation. I never burdened myself with 'Why me?' questions. After all, why *not* me? Even when things were at their worst, I remained aware that this was not permanent; it was not happening *to me*. It was just happening."

Now fully embracing his new life, Allan echoes the words I've heard from other survivors of serious illness and great trauma. He speaks with gratitude for the lessons learned and wisdom gained in the new life that opened up for him. "I wouldn't be willing to give up all the good that has come out of this for anything," he told me. Allan's courage lay in fully accepting and absorbing the lessons of this life-altering challenge, and moving into a new future with renewed resolve and determination.

THE BEAUTY OF THE SOUL
SHINES OUT
WHEN A MAN BEARS WITH COMPOSURE
ONE HEAVY MISCHANCE AFTER ANOTHER,
NOT BECAUSE HE DOES NOT FEEL THEM,
BUT BECAUSE HE IS A MAN
OF HIGH AND HEROIC TEMPER.

ARISTOTLE

"A further sign of health is that we don't become

undone by fear and trembling but we take it as a message that it's

time to stop struggling and look directly at what's threatening us.

Things like disappointment and anxiety are messengers telling

us that we're about to go into unknown territory."

PEMA CHÖDRÖN

PATIENCE AND FORTITUDE CONQUER EVERYTHING.

RALPH WALDO EMERSON

COURAGE

Courage is the price that Life
exacts for granting peace.
The soul that knows it not,
knows no release
 from little things:

Knows not the livid loneliness of fear,
Nor mountain heights where bitter joy
can hear
The sound of wings.

Now can Life grant us boon of living,
compensate
For gray dull ugliness and pregnant hate
Unless we dare
The soul's dominion? Each time we make a choice, we pay
With courage to behold the resistless day,
And count it fair.

AMELIA EARHART

"If you can descend to your rock bottom,

no matter what brings you there, you will find God's river.

And, at the place of crossing, if you put down all that you carry,

if you send on all that you love, if naked of all attachment you wait

in your deepest rock through your darkest night, the spirit of the

Universe will enfold you, and you will have the chance of a lifetime

to turn and bend, to wrestle with the elusive Being of the World.

Then, if you can hold on until there is a trace of fresh light, the

ineffable will reveal itself to you, and that revelation will bless you,

renew you, enable you to wade through God's river into the

freshness of original living."

MARK NEPO

"I think we spend so much of our lives

trying to pretend that we know what's going to happen

next. In fact we don't. To recognize that we don't know even

what will happen this afternoon and yet having the courage

to move forward—that's one meaning of faith."

SHARON SALZBERG

TO HAVE COURAGE FOR WHATEVER COMES IN LIFE— EVERYTHING LIES IN THAT.

SAINT TERESA OF AVILA

WHO SEES ALL BEINGS

IN HIS OWN SELF,

AND HIS OWN SELF IN ALL BEINGS,

LOSES ALL FEAR.

WHEN A SAGE SEES THIS

GREAT UNITY AND HIS SELF

HAS BECOME ALL BEINGS,

WHAT DELUSION AND WHAT SORROW

CAN EVER BE NEAR HIM?

ISHA UPANISHAD

UNNATURAL STATE OF THE UNICORN

Introduce me first as a man.
Don't mention superficial laurels
the dead heap up on the living.
I am a man. Cut me & I bleed.
Before embossed limited editions,
before fat artichoke hearts marinated
in rich sauce & served with imported wines,
before antics & Agnus Dei,
before the stars in your eyes
mean birth sign or Impression,
I am a man. I've scuffled
in mudholes, broken teeth in a grinning skull
like the moon behind bars. I've done it all
to be known as myself. No titles.
I have principles. I won't speak
on the natural state of the unicorn
in literature or self-analysis.

I have no birthright to prove,
no insignia, no secret
password, no fleur-de-lis.
My initials aren't on a branding iron.
I'm standing here in unpolished
shoes & faded jeans, sweating
my manly sweat. Inside my skin,
loving you, I am the space
my body believes in.

YUSEF KOMUNYAKAA

COURAGE

IS BEING SCARED TO DEATH

AND SADDLING UP ANYWAY.

JOHN WAYNE

> "BEING DEEPLY LOVED BY SOMEONE GIVES YOU STRENGTH,
> WHILE LOVING SOMEONE DEEPLY GIVES YOU COURAGE."
>
> ATTRIBUTED TO LAO TZU

Debi Jackson

DEBI JACKSON is a conservative Southern Baptist Republican from Alabama—on paper, at least, she's not the kind of woman you'd expect to be particularly open and receptive when her three-year-old son told her that he was actually a girl. But parental love, and the courage it makes possible, can surprise us in the most remarkable ways.

At the age of three, Debi's then son, AJ, asked for a princess dress. Thrilled by how it made him feel, AJ wanted to wear it everywhere. Soon he was asking for more and more girls' clothing. At age four, he told Debi, "You know, I'm really a girl, right? I'm a girl on the inside." He expressed increasing distress with his genitals, wanting them "gone."

Not knowing what to do about AJ's insistence that he was a girl, Debi and her husband tried to talk him out of going to school in girls' clothing. AJ grew sullen, angry, and depressed, and began biting and talking about suicide. Seeing their child's despair, but not having any real understanding of what it means to be transgender, Debi and her husband eventually decided to allow AJ to dress as a female and be considered a girl. Speaking with me about their decision, Debi shuns all praise for doing the "right thing." Her struggle, she says, was ultimately resolved by "seeing the distress in my child's face. She is the courageous one."

Transformed overnight into a happy child who called herself Sparkles, AJ had been set free by her parents' love and their courage to follow her lead. At school, teachers and children were universally accepting and affectionate. Once the children went home and told their parents, however, it was a different story. Debi and her husband were rejected by their fellow parents and even by some family members, and lost nearly all their friends. They were assaulted by a barrage of hurtful criticisms of them as parents and as human beings.

Knowing that they were dealing with a situation in which they had no experience or expertise, the Jacksons began to research what it means to be a transgender child. They read everything they could find, searched the Internet and joined groups of parents of trans children, and consulted psychiatrists, counselors, and physicians. Their immersion in this world allowed them to see AJ as one of many others who present the hallmarks, as the literature says, of "insistently, consistently, and persistently" maintaining that they are truly the opposite gender from the one indicated by their anatomy. The bottom line for Debi was, "She knows she is a girl, and that is good enough for me." Sparkles was now allowed to be the girl she intuitively knew she was; four years later, she gives every indication of being a happy and well-adjusted eight-year-old.

From the moment we become parents, we wonder how we would handle all manner of situations for which there are no clear-cut answers. Even the most supportive and loving parents can suddenly latch onto rigid ideas and rules when confronting unexpected challenges, in the misguided belief that they are serving their children in the best way they know how. Some people become fearful about how an "unusual" child reflects on them. It is the rare parent who can enter into completely foreign territory, intuitively trust their child's internal compass, and let love and courage lead the way.

Part of this new territory for Debi has been speaking out publicly about her experience, in hopes of helping other parents and children navigate a complex journey that is far too often filled with pain and fear. A soft-spoken woman who is unaccustomed to drawing attention to herself, Debi is now an active spokesperson for trans children, and the founder of Trans-Parenting, an organization dedicated to providing support and educational resources to parents and their advocates. She has created an open forum for communication and discussion that did not exist even a few years ago. Debi's stirring 2014 speech at the Unity Temple in Kansas City, which has gone viral on YouTube, is a moving call for parents to rise, with grace and courage, to even the most extraordinary needs of their children. Debi Jackson embodies courage in the service of love.

DEEP DOWN
IN THE HUMAN SPIRIT
THERE IS A RESERVOIR
OF COURAGE.
IT IS ALWAYS AVAILABLE,
ALWAYS WAITING TO BE
DISCOVERED.

PEMA CHÖDRÖN

FEARLESSNESS
IS NOT ONLY POSSIBLE,
IT IS THE ULTIMATE JOY.

WHEN YOU TOUCH NONFEAR,
YOU ARE FREE.

THICH NHAT HANH

BE BOLD

AND MIGHTY FORCES
WILL COME TO YOUR AID.

GOETHE

BEDECKED

Tell me it's wrong the scarlet nails my son sports or the toy
store rings he clusters four jewels to each finger.

He's bedecked. I see the other mothers looking at the star
choker, the rhinestone strand he fastens over a sock.
Sometimes I help him find sparkle clip-ons when he says
sticker earrings look too fake.

Tell me I should teach him it's wrong to love the glitter that a
boy's only a boy who'd love a truck with a remote that revs,
battery slamming into corners or Hot Wheels loop-de-looping
off tracks into the tub.

Then tell me it's fine—really—maybe even a good thing—a boy
who's got some girl to him,
and I'm right for the days he wears a pink shirt on the seesaw in
the park.

Tell me what you need to tell me but keep far away from my son
who still loves a beautiful thing not for what it means—
this way or that—but for the way facets set off prisms and
prisms spin up everywhere
and from his own jeweled body he's cast rainbows—made every
shining true color.

Now try to tell me—man or woman—your heart was ever once
that brave.

VICTORIA REDEL

HAPPY ARE THOSE WHO DARE COURAGEOUSLY TO DEFEND WHAT THEY LOVE.

OVID

WHO COULD REFRAIN
THAT HAD A HEART TO LOVE
AND IN THAT HEART
COURAGE TO MAKE
LOVE KNOWN?

SHAKESPEARE

TO A MILKWEED

Teach me to love what I've made, and judgment
in that love.

Teach me your arrogance.
With each five-petaled horned flower teach me

how much blossoming matters

                      along roadsides, dry-

beds, these fields no longer cleared.
Teach me such patience at each turning, how

to live on nothing but will, its milky
juices, poison

to the others, though when its stem is broken,
bleeds. Teach me to

need the future,

            and the past, that Indian summer.

Let me be tricked into believing
that by what moves in me I might be saved,

and hold to this. Hold
onto this until there's wind enough.

DEBORAH DIGGES

THE SERENITY PRAYER

GOD GRANT ME:

SERENITY TO ACCEPT THE

THINGS I CANNOT CHANGE,

COURAGE TO CHANGE THE

THINGS I CAN & WISDOM

TO KNOW THE DIFFERENCE.

REINHOLD NIEBUHR

> ## "YOU CAN'T TEST COURAGE CAUTIOUSLY."
>
> ANNIE DILLARD

Amani Mirielle Kahatwa

WHEN WE HEAR young children speak of what profession they envision for themselves, we often dismiss it as youthful fantasy. With some young people (such as Gaby Hernandez, whose story is on page 184) the mission of their lives is clear and unshakable very early on.

Amani Kahatwa has always known that she wanted to use her voice to speak up for the voiceless. Despite challenge, risk, and great danger, the courage of this determined activist manages to balance acknowledgment of the difficult reality around her with unblinking determination to boldly live her life's mission.

In 2006, the UN Security Council passed UN Resolution 1820, stating that rape and other forms of sexual violence can now constitute war crimes. Before this resolution, such acts were simply considered collateral damage. This resolution demands the prosecution of an entirely new form of crime, as well as a new understanding of rape as a strategic weapon whose goal is to destroy not just the individual victim but also her family, community, and culture. In the context of war, rape is now equated with genocide. Experts in the field agree that we have only just begun to grapple with the enormity of this type of crime in war zones throughout the world.

For some time, the Democratic Republic of Congo (DRC) has been regarded as the epicenter of the crisis of rape as a weapon of war, the place the UN calls "the rape capital of the world." More than five million have died in civil wars in the region since 1994. The Eastern DRC has become especially infamous for particularly traumatic physical consequences of rape. It was the norm for perpetrators to use guns, knives, and bayonets to rupture the bodies of victims—some of whom were as young as eleven months. The physical damage is horrifying and the psychological, social, and spiritual scars indelible.

In response to the crisis, the Chicago-based American Bar Association has established a one-room office in the HEAL Africa hospital in Goma, part of the Democratic Republic of Congo, flanked on either side by offices providing the psychological and spiritual counseling that rape victims require in order for their healing to begin. In the central office sits the remarkable young Congolese lawyer Amani Mirielle Kahatwa, who heads the USAID-funded program that is charged with prosecuting these crimes in a country the size of all of Western Europe.

Ferociously committed to her work, Amani outlines the task at hand: "Congolese law is perfect. The laws on the books are impeccable. The problem is implementation." The other problem is impunity. Some perpetrators can't be found. Still others remain in positions of power. Most women are afraid of being harassed, harmed, or killed if they step forward. Amani shows them how to fight back as she stands in front of uniformed officers claiming that they are rapists, not liberators. She feels the women's fear and frustration and is their strongest advocate: "Women have had enough of these things happening. They want this to end." Despite persistent intimidation and continual death threats, she remains on the front lines, representing the women in this fight and showing them that they are all victims of crimes now worthy of prosecution and conviction.

Over seven days in February of 2014, in the market town of Minova, on the shore of Lake Kivu in eastern Congo, thirty-nine soldiers were brought to trial for rapes committed over a ten-day scourge of violence in November 2012. More than one thousand men, women, and children were raped in this town alone. Only forty-seven testified. All but four of the accused soldiers sat in the trial room housed in the auditorium of the local Catholic school. Women brave enough to confront their rapists but still fearful of consequences to themselves and their families testified while covered in veils and behind screens. In Amani's skilled hands, this one trial resulted in twenty-seven convictions.

With State Department funding, lawyers in the region have interviewed 250 victims and pursued more than one hundred cases. In eleven months, they received thirty judgments with sentences of five to twenty years. The process is, quite literally, never-ending, and these trials are only the beginning. But the work has a remarkable champion in Amani Kahatwa.

Like many of the heroes in this book, Amani does not speak of her work as extraordinary. She simply sees this as what needs to be done—work that has been put in her path and to which she is dedicated. A lawyer for ten years, she could have chosen any number of avenues to pursue in her profession. The need for lawyers in the Congo is immense. But she has always known her calling: "As I grew up in an environment in which women and children were completely marginalized, I always felt called to uphold their rights to say *no* to discrimination and violence to all people. This opportunity to represent the women of the Congo in their struggle has emboldened me. My courage lies in service to them."

The risks she faces every day are of a different order from what most of us can imagine. Aware of the dangers, she remains focused on the daily work of getting victims to go on, recover, speak out, return to their villages. Her powerful voice and her courage in speaking truth to power, demanding justice, and protecting the innocent, day after day, are the focus of the soon-to-be-released documentary film *The Prosecutors*. "Many women and girls don't know their rights," she says. "This is my contribution in the fight against ignorance among women and children. I consider myself their voice."

COURAGE IS GRACE UNDER PRESSURE.

ERNEST HEMINGWAY

ANY INTELLIGENT FOOL

CAN MAKE THINGS BIGGER,

MORE COMPLEX, AND MORE VIOLENT.

IT TAKES A TOUCH OF GENIUS—

AND A LOT OF COURAGE—

TO MOVE IN THE

OPPOSITE DIRECTION.

E. F. SCHUMACHER

COURAGE MEANS
BEING ABLE TO ACT
IN THE MIDST OF FEAR.

JOSEPH GOLDSTEIN

ENCOURAGEMENT

MEANS TO PLANT THE SEED OF

COURAGE IN THE LIVES OF OTHERS.

IT IS AN ACT OF

REGENERATION.

DAISAKU IKEDA

NOT HERE

There's courage involved if you want
to become truth.

There is a broken-open place in a lover.

Where are those qualities of bravery and
sharp compassion in this group? What's the
use of old and frozen thought?

I want a howling hurt. This is not a treasury
where gold is stored; this is for copper.

We alchemists look for talent that
can heat up and change.

Lukewarm won't do. Halfhearted holding back,
well-enough getting by? Not here.

RUMI

"Faith . . . is crumpling and throwing away everything, proposition by proposition, until nothing is left, and then writing a new proposition, your very own, to throw in the teeth of despair."

MARY JEAN IRION

THE ONLY SERVICE

A FRIEND CAN REALLY RENDER

IS TO KEEP UP YOUR COURAGE

BY HOLDING UP TO YOU A MIRROR

IN WHICH YOU CAN SEE

A NOBLE IMAGE OF

YOURSELF.

GEORGE BERNARD SHAW

THE BEST PROTECTION

ANY WOMAN CAN HAVE...

Is COURAGE.

ELIZABETH CADY STANTON

FROM CARING COMES COURAGE.

ANONYMOUS

I GIVE YOU BACK

I release you, my beautiful and terrible
fear. I release you. You were my beloved
and hated twin, but now, I don't know you
as myself. I release you with all the
pain I would know at the death of
my children.

You are not my blood anymore.

I give you back to the soldiers
who burned down my house, beheaded my children,
raped and sodomized my brothers and sisters.
I give you back to those who stole the
food from our plates when we were starving.

I release you, fear, because you hold
these scenes in front of me and I was born
with eyes that can never close.

I release you
I release you
I release you
I release you

I am not afraid to be angry.
I am not afraid to rejoice.
I am not afraid to be black.
I am not afraid to be white.
I am not afraid to be hungry.
I am not afraid to be full.
I am not afraid to be hated.
I am not afraid to be loved.
to be loved, to be loved, fear.

Oh, you have choked me, but I gave you the leash.
You have gutted me but I gave you the knife.
You have devoured me, but I laid myself across the fire.

I take myself back, fear.

You are not my shadow any longer.

I won't hold you in my hands.

You can't live in my eyes, my ears, my voice

my belly, or in my heart my heart

my heart my heart

But come here, fear

I am alive and you are so afraid

of dying.

JOY HARJO

> "THE OPPOSITE FOR COURAGE IS NOT COWARDICE,
> IT IS CONFORMITY. EVEN A DEAD FISH
> CAN GO WITH THE FLOW."
>
> JIM HIGHTOWER

Larry Yang

I HAVE BELIEVED FOR some time that there can often be great courage in a life of committed spiritual practice. We hear of the Dalai Lama's rising each day at 3:00 a.m. in order to devote most of the morning hours to meditation before turning to the concerns of his millions of followers. Likewise, we look at the contemplative prayer that guides Pope Francis. And there are the quiet lives of devoted, rigorous spiritual practice that we rarely hear about—those that are unfolding in the remote monasteries of distant continents and also on America's city streets and small towns.

Buddhist teacher Larry Yang's life is one of quiet, determined courage. Larry was born to Chinese parents who immigrated to Ohio in the McCarthy years of the early 1950s. Growing up gay and Chinese, he always felt like an outsider in mainstream American life. "I have been 'other' or different for most of my life," he says. But, rather than letting himself be held back by this, Larry embraced it, with an early determination to "do better than mainstream culture."

This determination did not always make for an easy path. Larry's young adult years were marked by discrimination and addictions of various kinds. He describes himself at that time as "craving to be someone who I was not, craving for happiness that I didn't have, craving for the suffering of internalized oppression, racism, and homophobia to cease, and medicating all of that suffering with drugs and alcohol, which I didn't realize were additional arrows of suffering."

We have all heard similar stories; some of us have lived them. These experiences can break us or save us. In Larry's case, they led him to meditation and, ultimately, Buddhist study and practice. It was a transformational step in which he discovered his life's work.

"As I practiced, I began to realize that my experience was not personal to me—that many people probably were having the same experience of exclusion and dismissal within the dominant cultural interpretation of the Dharma," he reflects. "That was the seed of my future teaching—that the door into freedom was ironically through the experience of identity, which was counter-indicative to what most mainstream teachers were teaching, and still do. My own experience is that I continue, through the specifics of my identity, to see, feel, and experience what is beyond it. I practice through the particulars to connect to the universal."

Larry is now a beloved Buddhist teacher and founder of the East Bay Meditation Center in downtown Oakland, California. Dedicated to holding diversity as a core principle, the center is home to a vibrant community that includes many members of the LGBTQ and other minority populations. It's bursting at the seams with more than 150 volunteers, and hosts a full schedule of classes taught by noted teachers from around the world. Nothing like it exists in the country.

In order to break this new ground in a very established culture, Larry had to look for empowerment in the American Buddhist world—something that was not easy to come by. But he swam upstream, upheld the need for this unique dharma community in the face of disapproval and disinterest, and prevailed. Because of Larry's activist work and the efforts of other leaders, the field of "engaged Buddhism" has changed the landscape of this contemplative study and practice to one in and of the world, on the front lines of activism in social justice and environmental action, and representing the issues of the world's diverse populations.

As he tells me about the success of the center, Larry remembers a pivotal story from his childhood. At around age seven, he was playing in his neighborhood and noticed a little girl several years younger who was being bullied. He walked up to the older and bigger boys who were taunting her, and said, "How would it be if somebody treated you like that?" Then he took her hand and walked her home. Others had been looking on, but nobody else had stepped in to offer help. With no particular fanfare, Larry sums up the effect of the experience on his life today: "That is the work I do now."

Determination, humility, integrity, patience, love, and caring for the world. This is Larry Yang's recipe for a courageous life, one that continuously inspires his students and shines like a beacon for the community he has created. To speak with Larry is to hear a heart on fire for courageously creating, supporting, and sustaining communities that both represent and respond to many of our world's most pressing struggles.

"If your everyday practice is to open to all

your emotions, to all the people you meet, to all the situations

you encounter, without closing down, trusting that you can do

that—then that will take you as far as you can go. And then you

will understand all the teachings that anyone has ever taught."

PEMA CHÖDRÖN

WITH ENOUGH COURAGE, YOU CAN DO WITHOUT A REPUTATION.

RHETT BUTLER

EVERY MAN OF COURAGE
IS A MAN OF HIS WORD.

PIERRE CORNEILLE

"Whatever you do, you need courage.

Whatever course you decide upon, there is always someone

to tell you that you are wrong. There are always difficulties

arising that tempt you to believe your critics are right. To map

out a course of action and to follow it to an end requires some

of the same courage that a soldier needs. Peace has its victories,

but it takes brave men and women to win them."

ANONYMOUS,
VARIOUSLY ATTRIBUTED

THE INVITATION

It doesn't interest me
if the story you are telling me
is true.
I want to know if you can
disappoint another
to be true to yourself.
If you can bear
the accusation of betrayal
and not betray your own soul.
If you can be faithless
and therefore trustworthy.

I want to know if you can see Beauty
even when it is not pretty
every day.

And if you can source your own life
from its presence.

I want to know
if you can live with failure
yours and mine
and still stand at the edge of the lake
and shout to the silver of the full moon,
„Yes."

It doesn't interest me
to know where you live
or how much money you have.
I want to know if you can get up
after the night of grief and despair
weary and bruised to the bone

and do what needs to be done
to feed the children.

It doesn't interest me
who you know
or how you came to be here.
I want to know if you will stand
in the center of the fire with me
and not shrink back.

It doesn't interest me
where or what or with whom
you have studied.
I want to know
what sustains you
from the inside
when all else falls away.

I want to know

if you can be alone

with yourself

and if you truly like

the company you keep

in the empty moments.

ORIAH MOUNTAIN DREAMER

HOW FEW THERE ARE
WHO HAVE COURAGE ENOUGH
TO OWN THEIR FAULTS,
OR RESOLUTION ENOUGH
TO MEND THEM.

BENJAMIN FRANKLIN

"Getting started on a spiritual path takes guts.

We usually don't know it in the beginning, but if we keep going

on it—if we really want to know the truth of what it means to be

human or if we are deeply finished with our suffering—we will

learn that walking the path of freedom takes a humble courage."

TEAH STROZER

"*Courage* is the measure of our heartfelt

participation with life, with another, with a community, a work;

a future. To be courageous, is not necessarily to go anywhere or

do anything except to make conscious those things we already feel

deeply and then to live through the unending vulnerabilities of those

consequences. To be courageous is to seat our feelings deeply in

the body and in the world: to live up to and into the necessities

of relationships that often already exist, with things we find we

already care deeply about: with a person, a future, a possibility in

society, or with an unknown that begs us on and always has begged

us on. To be *courageous* is to stay close to the way we are made."

DAVID WHYTE

ONE WHO CONQUERS

HIMSELF

IS GREATER THAN ANOTHER

WHO CONQUERS

A THOUSAND TIMES

A THOUSAND

ON THE BATTLEFIELD.

THE BUDDHA

ON QUITTING

How much grit do you think you've got?
Can you quit a thing that you like a lot?
You may talk of pluck; it's an easy word,
And where'er you go it is often heard;
But can you tell to a jot or guess
Just how much courage you now possess?

You may stand to trouble and keep your grin,
But have you tackled self-discipline?
Have you ever issued commands to you
To quit the things that you like to do,
And then, when tempted and sorely swayed,
Those rigid orders have you obeyed?

Don't boast of your grit till you've tried it out,
Nor prate to men of your courage stout,
For it's easy enough to retain a grin
In the face of a fight there's a chance to win,

But the sort of grit that is good to own

Is the stuff you need when you're all alone.

How much grit do you think you've got?

Can you turn from joys that you like a lot?

Have you ever tested yourself to know

How far with yourself your will can go?

If you want to know if you have grit,

Just pick out a joy that you like, and quit.

It's bully sport and it's open fight;

It will keep you busy both day and night;

For the toughest kind of a game you'll find

Is to make your body obey your mind.

And you never will know what is meant by grit

Unless there's something you've tried to quit.

EDGAR ALBERT GUEST

"COURAGE IS KNOWING WHAT NOT TO FEAR."

PLATO

Nazila Fathi

THE SEEDS OF a courageous life are sometimes found in surprisingly peaceful beginnings. Such was the early life of Nazila Fathi, born in 1970 into a comfortably well-off and loving family in Iran's capital city, Tehran.

Everything changed overnight for Nazila and her family in 1979, with the exile of the Shah and the sudden ascent to power of Ayatollah Khomeini. Her carefree childhood came to a screeching halt. Everyone had to publicly conform to obligatory Islamic dress and profess strict religious beliefs, as well as allegiance to the new regime—even Nazila and her third-grade classmates. Her father, formerly a high-ranking member of the Ministry of Energy, lost his job under the new regime, essentially for wearing a tie and speaking English. He was forced to work in an orchard to support his family, while the family's housekeeper, who supported Khomeini, was now able to retire and buy a large apartment. A family friend had faced the firing squad for his opposition to the regime, while others had simply disappeared. As Nazila said, "It was as if there had been a calm music until then, and now a new song began: the drumbeats of the new regime."

From the age of nine, Nazila felt the shadow of perpetual danger—remote at times, and then terrifyingly close—as a palpable presence. The ensuing years of Iran's war with Iraq (1980–88) brought bombs and great deprivation to the family's doorstep.

Throughout these years, she persevered with her education, studying English at Azad University and ultimately becoming a translator for foreign journalists in Iran. Bitten by the journalism bug in 1992 while covering a campaign event, she eventually became a distinguished journalist, publishing more than two thousand articles in the *New York Times* as well as writing for *Time* magazine and Agence France-Presse. Working with international reporters uncovering the reality of the situation in Iran ultimately became perilous. "I knew that I would be putting myself at risk," she recalls. Nazila's particular form of courage was in unflinchingly bearing witness to the inequity, pain, and suffering in her country. As the situation worsened over the years and other reporters fled and were imprisoned, her passionate dedication to portraying the real Iran to the outside world only increased. By 2005, she was under surveillance by the Intelligence Ministry and Revolutionary Guards, and she eventually discovered that her housekeeper was a spy reporting on her every movement. Yet she chose to persist.

In the summer of 2009, when she was reporting on increasing tensions, intimidations, arrests, and violence against peaceful protesters, a senior official warned her that, in response to the government's ban on reporting on the protests, "the government forces have given your photo to snipers with orders to shoot you. Stop going out on the streets." A reporter to the core, Nazila had a simple, clear, and fearless response: "My neighbors [with their protests] were making history and I wanted to witness it. I had no idea the act of bearing witness would change my life forever."

But bearing witness was what had defined her life and, once again, she persisted, now as the only *Times* reporter remaining in Iran. She says of the time, "Somehow my fear had evaporated."

Soon a phalanx of sixteen men began watching her building around the clock. Despite her courageous commitment to truth telling, Nazila now had to put the safety of her family first. As the surveillance team took a midnight break on July 1, 2009, Nazila, her husband, and their two young children fled to the airport, carrying only one small bag. Miraculously, after a lengthy, hostile interrogation, they made it through security and were able to head to a new life, first in Toronto and then in the United States. Nazila has not been able to return to Iran since that night.

By any measure, Nazila's final days in Iran and her flight to freedom qualify as courageous. They were the natural evolution of a life lived courageously; the strength and resolve that allowed her to persist in shining a spotlight on injustice and human rights abuse had been implanted in her early on and defined her.

In her moving memoir, *The Lonely War: One Woman's Account of the Struggle for Modern Iran,* Nazila modestly describes her mission throughout these years as simply "remaining conscious and sensible every time I was consumed by despair"—a very clear-eyed and down-to-earth definition of courage. And she praises her inspiring colleagues, friends, family, and her parents, whom she thanks for giving her the "wings to fly"—perhaps a more poetic description of the courage she embodies.

COURAGE IS

GETTING AWAY FROM DEATH

BY CONTINUALLY COMING

WITHIN AN INCH OF IT.

G. K. CHESTERTON

THE MOST COURAGEOUS ACT

IS STILL TO

THINK FOR YOURSELF.

ALOUD.

COCO CHANEL

FACED WITH WHAT IS RIGHT,

TO LEAVE IT UNDONE SHOWS

A LACK OF COURAGE.

CONFUCIUS

EVERYONE HAS TALENT.
WHAT IS RARE
IS THE COURAGE TO
FOLLOW THE TALENT TO
THE DARK PLACE
WHERE IT LEADS.

ERICA JONG

THE GRASP OF YOUR HAND

Let me not pray to be sheltered from dangers
but to be fearless in facing them.

Let me not beg for the stilling of my pain
but for the heart to conquer it.

Let me not look for allies in life's battlefield
but to my own strength.

Let me not crave in anxious fear to be saved
but hope for the patience to win my freedom.

Grant that I may not be a coward,
feeling Your mercy in my success alone;

But let me find the grasp of Your hand in my failure.

RABINDRANATH TAGORE

"Fearlessness may be a gift but perhaps

more precious is the courage . . . that comes from cultivating

the habit of refusing to let fear dictate one's actions.

AUNG SAN SUU KYI

REAL COURAGE

IS WHEN YOU KNOW

YOU'RE LICKED BEFORE YOU BEGIN

BUT YOU BEGIN ANYWAY

AND SEE IT THROUGH

NO MATTER WHAT.

HARPER LEE

"You gain strength, courage, and confidence

by every experience in which you really stop to look fear in the face.

You are able to say to yourself, 'I lived through this horror.

I can take the next thing that comes along.'"

ELEANOR ROOSEVELT

COURAGE IN DANGER IS HALF THE BATTLE.

TITUS MACCIUS PLAUTUS

MAGGID

The courage to let go of the door, the handle.
The courage to shed the familiar walls whose very
stains and leaks are comfortable as the little moles
of the upper arm; stains that recall a feast,
a child's naughtiness, a loud blattering storm
that slapped the roof hard, pouring through.

The courage to abandon the graves dug into the hill,
the small bones of children and the brittle bones
of the old whose marrow hunger had stolen;
the courage to desert the tree planted and only
begun to bear; the riverside where promises were
shaped; the street where their empty pots were broken.

The courage to leave the place whose language you learned
as early as your own, whose customs however dangerous or demeaning, bind you like a halter

you have learned to pull inside, to move your load;

the land fertile with the blood spilled on it;

the roads mapped and annotated for survival.

The courage to walk out of the pain that is known

into the pain that cannot be imagined,

mapless, walking into the wilderness, going

barefoot with a canteen into the desert;

stuffed in the stinking hold of a rotting ship

sailing off the map into dragons' mouths,

Cathay, India, Siberia, goldeneh medina

leaving bodies by the way like abandoned treasure.

So they walked out of Egypt. So they bribed their way

out of Russia under loads of straw; so they steamed

out of the bloody smoking charnelhouse of Europe

on overloaded freighters forbidden all ports—

out of pain into death or freedom or a different
painful dignity, into squalor and politics.
We Jews are all born of wanderers, with shoes
under our pillows and a memory of blood that is ours
raining down. We honor only those Jews who changed
tonight, those who chose the desert over bondage,

who walked into the strange and became strangers
and gave birth to children who could look down
on them standing on their shoulders for having
been slaves. We honor those who let go of everything but freedom, who ran, who revolted, who fought,
who became other by saving themselves.

MARGE PIERCY

I would define true courage to be

a perfect sensibility of the measure of danger,

and a mental willingness to endure it.

WILLIAM TECUMSEH SHERMAN

COURAGE IS

THE ART OF BEING

THE ONLY ONE

WHO KNOWS YOU'RE

SCARED TO DEATH.

EARL WILSON

REVELATION MUST BE TERRIBLE

Revelation must be
   terrible with no time left
to say goodbye.

Imagine that moment
   staring at the still waters
with only the brief tremor

of your body to say
   you are leaving everything
and everyone you know behind.

Being far from home is hard, but
   you know,
     at least we are exiled together.
When you open your eyes to the
   world

you are on your own for
   the first time. No one is
even interested in saving you now

and the world steps in
   to test the calm fluidity of your
     body
from moment to moment

as if it believed you could join
   its vibrant dance
of fire and calmness and final
   stillness.

As if you were meant to be exactly
   where you are, as if
like the dark branch of a desert
   river

you could flow on without a speck
    of guilt and everything
everywhere would still be just as it should be.

As if your place in the world mattered
    and the world could
neither speak nor hear the fullness of

its own bitter and beautiful cry
    without the deep well
of your body resonating in the echo.

Knowing that it takes only
    that one, terrible
word to make the circle complete,

revelation must be terrible
    knowing you can
never hide your voice again.

DAVID WHYTE

"WE MUST CONSTANTLY BUILD DIKES OF COURAGE TO HOLD BACK THE FLOOD OF FEAR."

MARTIN LUTHER KING, JR.

Jean Clarke-Mitchell

WE HAVE ALL heard too many stories of what has now become an epidemic of domestic abuse in our country and throughout the world. There is often such a blurring sameness to so many of these stories that we can become immune to hearing the individual voices of women and their children fighting for their lives. Each story can blend into the next. And yet each story is unique. The powerful thread that runs through so many of them is the extraordinary courage that these legions of women are able to summon up to save their own lives and the lives of their children, and then to move into a new life they had only dared imagine.

Jean Clarke-Mitchell serves as director of clinical services at the remarkable Elizabeth Freeman Center in Pittsfield, Massachusetts, an institution that helps survivors of sexual and domestic violence. Every day, Jean counsels women in abusive relationships, some searching for ways to escape and others living in denial, hoping that things will work out if they just hang in there.

What makes Jean the ideal person for this role is the fact that, twenty-one years ago, she walked the same courageous path that she supports others in navigating today. Jean's story is her own. But it is also that of millions of women around the world, many of whose circumstances do not allow them the option to leave.

A sixty-year-old woman of model-like beauty and poise, Jean grew up in Jamaica, in a large family of extremely humble circumstances. But her parents always gave her a sense of being extraordinary. She was continually acknowledged for her intelligence and beauty. Though her family could not afford it, she navigated her own determined path to education at an exclusive private school that would open the wider world to her.

After coming to the United States, Jean attended college, where she met and married her husband, who was studying to be an electrical engineer. It gradually became clear that she was married to a very controlling man who, eventually, after the birth of their two children, became verbally and physically abusive. Living in the denial that is common to most victims of abuse, Jean held out hope for four years that life would change for the better, before realizing that her only choice was to leave. She spoke with a local women's hotline referral service to find a shelter to which she and her two children could move.

One day, after her husband left for work, she loaded her children and two small bags into her tiny car and headed to a city an hour away, where they could live safely and anonymously. In the ensuing days, her new advisors took her back to her hometown to obtain a year-long order of protection, the key document that would allow her to embark on a new life.

Knowing no one in her new community, Jean immediately focused on the task of getting her children into the best possible school. Drawing on her own childhood experience, she found her way to the region's most exclusive school, applying for admission for her children a few weeks before school was to start, with no job or source of income.

But her determination that her unusually bright children should have the best education possible made her fearless. They were both admitted on scholarship and started their school year being picked up by the school bus at the women's shelter—a location few, if any, of their classmates had ever seen or heard about.

Within six weeks, Jean had found an apartment for them and work for herself. Her new life had begun. Jean's work focused on helping women in abusive relationships, answering the hotline at the center where she first lived, and studying social work. She finished her bachelor's degree, master's degree in social work, and the coursework for her PhD, earning straight As all the way through. The Elizabeth Freeman Center has now been her professional home for two decades.

There are no stereotypes for women in abusive relationships. Jean's clients run the gamut from those with no resources of any kind to distinguished lawyers and doctors, pillars of the community. But they often share a penchant for denying that this relationship, into which they once poured so much hope and love, has become impossibly dangerous. And they all share self-recrimination for having missed the signs, and even for having loved this person in the first place. Denial and shame are not ingredients that always lead to courage but, in the lives of victims of abuse, they can prove to be its wake-up call.

Victims of abuse often marry handsome, successful charmers, those whom no one would suspect of this tragic flaw. For many women, their courage, strength, and independence are what draw these needy men to them in the first place and, when their narcissism is punctured, they lash out.

Many of these women share Jean's courage to embrace the often sudden realization that life is precious and not to be squandered, that it is up to them to give their children love and security, and that they are able to take on huge risks to make it happen. There are those who don't survive embarking on a new life. Others are too frightened to attempt it. And some, like Jean, embrace their own strength, and find the courage to create the life they come to believe they deserve. It is their courage that serves as the inspiration for countless others. Jean not only lives a courageous life, but also serves as an example of courage for everyone whose life she touches.

COME TO THE EDGE

Come to the edge.

We might fall.

Come to the edge.

It's too high!

COME TO THE EDGE!

And they came,

And he pushed,

And they flew.

CHRISTOPHER LOGUE

FATE LOVES THE FEARLESS.

JAMES RUSSELL LOWELL

COURAGE DOESN'T ALWAYS

ROAR.

SOMETIMES COURAGE IS

THE QUIET VOICE

AT THE END OF THE DAY

SAYING,

"I WILL TRY AGAIN TOMORROW."

MARY ANNE RADMACHER

"For a long time, I felt I couldn't move

forward until fear was gone. But there were too many

challenges to simply stop moving and I realized there wasn't

any choice but to move forward and do what was necessary.

Rather than thinking I could only move when I had 'conquered'

fear, I learned to hold hands with fear and keep going."

KATHLEEN DOWLING SINGH

THE SECRET OF HAPPINESS

IS FREEDOM . . .

AND THE SECRET OF FREEDOM

IS COURAGE.

THUCYDIDES

SOME NOTES ON COURAGE

Think of a child who goes out
into the new neighborhood,
cap at an angle, and offers to lend
a baseball glove. He knows
how many traps there are—
his accent or his clothes, the club
already formed.
Think of a pregnant woman
whose first child died—
her history of blood.
Or your friend whose father
locked her in basements, closets,
cars. Now when she speaks
to strangers, she must have
all the windows open.
She forces herself indoors each day,
sheer will makes her climb the stairs.

And love. Imagine it. After all
those years in the circus, that last
bad fall when the net didn't hold.
Think of the ladder to the wire,
spotlights moving as you move,
then how you used to see yourself
balanced on the shiny air.
Think of doing it again.

SUSAN LUDVIGSON

"One isn't necessarily born with courage, but one is born with potential. Without courage, we cannot practice any other virtue with consistency. We can't be kind, true, merciful, generous, or honest."

MAYA ANGELOU

HAPPY ARE THOSE WHO

DARE COURAGEOUSLY

TO DEFEND WHAT THEY LOVE.

OVID

YOU'VE GOT TO

JUMP OFF THE CLIFF

ALL THE TIME

AND BUILD YOUR WINGS

ON THE WAY DOWN.

RAY BRADBURY

THE JOURNEY

One day you finally knew
what you had to do, and began,
though the voices around you
kept shouting
their bad advice—
though the whole house began to tremble
and you felt the old tug
at your ankles.
"Mind my life!"
each voice cried.
But you didn't stop.
You knew what you had to do,
though the wind pried
with its stiff fingers
at the very foundations—
though their melancholy

was terrible.
It was already late
enough, and a wild night
and the road full of fallen
branches and stones.
But little by little,
as you left their voices behind,
the stars began to burn
through the sheets of clouds
and there was a new voice,
which you slowly
recognized as your own
that kept you company
as you strode deeper and deeper
into the world,
determined to do
the only thing you could do—
determined to save
the only life that you could save.

MARY OLIVER

> "YOUR LIFE UNFOLDS IN PROPORTION
> TO YOUR COURAGE."
>
> ANONYMOUS

Gabriela Chavez Hernandez

WHEN WE SEE indomitable courage emerge in very young lives, it is hard to know how it took shape with so little worldly experience. Is courage inborn? Do some of us arrive with an extra measure? Or does it lie latent in all of us until a particular set of circumstances ignites it?

We have all stood in awe of teenage Nobel Prize winner Malala Yousafzai's story of nearly losing her life as she stood up for the right of Pakistani girls and women to an education, a cause that has become her life's work. Malala's early life was a modest one. But when her moment of trial arrived, she was ready to step forward. We can only imagine how many Malalas are living anonymous, unheralded lives in faraway parts of the globe, practicing the courage for a life of extraordinary meaning and selfless service.

Gaby Hernandez is one such young woman. When I met her, she was in the final weeks before her graduation from Sacred Heart University in Fairfield, Connecticut, with a major in business. But her journey to graduation day started far away, in a tiny, remote village, a bumpy three-hour drive into the mountains from Oaxaca, Mexico. Of her early influences, she speaks most passionately about her parents and grandparents, who always told her that, despite her surroundings, she had the ability to make something extraordinary of her life.

Gaby was five when she visited Oaxaca for the first time. She was profoundly struck by the sense of a different life awaiting her: "I knew there was a bigger world. I knew there was something better," she recalls. Knowing that she was holding that vision for herself, her grandparents taught her the Spanish she would need for a life in the city, insisting that she speak it at home rather than the local dialect.

Gaby's village offered no schooling beyond the fifth grade. It was the rare child who could find a way to continue her studies. But Gaby had decided that she wanted to become a doctor or a teacher, and she knew that her dream could only come true if she left her village. She had heard about a children's home in Oaxaca, and decided that was where she needed to be in order to find a school in the city. At age twelve, she arrived at the children's home, joining some forty others, mostly orphans and disabled. She cooked and cared for the children, and before long did the bookkeeping for the home as well.

Gaby knew nothing about city life. She was among strangers. At the school she attended, she was the only student who was an outsider, the only one not living with her family. She knew nothing of computers or the other basics of modern schooling. But Gaby has always had a special gift for, as she says, "finding good people." She found friends and formed relationships with devoted teachers and others who helped her. She remembers her determination to succeed in her new life, the same determination she had always carried with her: "I didn't think about challenges, just opportunities."

Over the ensuing years, Gaby formed friendships with the heads of the nonprofit

Simply Smiles, which was spearheading a project in the city to provide better futures for impoverished children, their families, and their communities. That connection led to their offer of a full scholarship for Gaby to attend college in the United States. She accepted without a moment's hesitation, despite how distant it was from anything she had known. "I wanted to demonstrate to the children there that it doesn't matter how you grow up if you have a chance to do something important," she says.

Denied her first visa application, Gaby appealed. When the authorities at the U.S. Consulate read her inspiring appeal, they invited her for a personal interview and, upon meeting her, granted the visa within minutes. Gaby likens that moment to "someone handing me a key to a new house." She left for Westport, Connecticut, two weeks later. It took her two years at a community college to learn enough English to complete her associate's degree and then transfer to Sacred Heart. Studying in an American university was filled with challenges, but she persevered. And now she prepares for graduation with a degree that will open doors seemingly unimaginable to that little girl in the mountain village.

Filled with gratitude for the unique gifts she had received, Gaby spent her American summers helping Simply Smiles in their groundbreaking work with the Cheyenne River Sioux tribe on their reservation in South Dakota. Nobody expected her to do this; it was simply in her nature to continue to open doors for others as they had been opened for her.

Gaby has boundless possibilities for building a future in the United States, but instead she has decided to return home to Oaxaca, where she will help build, establish, and manage a new children's home for the organization that sponsored her. She will serve as its first executive director, using her innate understanding of what these children want and need to help them meet their special challenges and give them the confidence to live the lives they yearn for. She also hopes to earn enough to give her youngest sister the opportunity to go to college, too. Gaby knows that returning to Mexico means giving up the opportunities offered by a life in the United States, but she is following her instincts, relying on her lifelong confidence that she is on the right path to fulfill her destiny to "do something big."

Gaby's special form of courage was born where determination, altruism, and faith meet. It has shaped and nurtured the beginning of what will undoubtedly be an extraordinary life whose mission is as a teacher of courage.

I AM NOT AFRAID OF STORMS

FOR I AM LEARNING HOW

TO SAIL MY SHIP.

LOUISA MAY ALCOTT

AS YOU GO THE WAY OF LIFE,

YOU WILL SEE A GREAT

CHASM:

JUMP.

IT IS NOT AS WIDE AS YOU

THINK.

NATIVE AMERICAN SAYING

IT TAKES COURAGE TO GROW UP AND BECOME WHO YOU REALLY ARE.

E. E. CUMMINGS

"To me, there is no greater act
of courage

than being the one who kisses first."

JANEANE GAROFALO

THE PUPIL

Picture me, the shy pupil at the door,
One small, tight fist clutching the dread Czerny.
Back then time was still harmony, not money,
And I could spend a whole week practicing for
That moment on the threshold.

                             Then to take courage,
And enter, and pass among mysterious scents,
And sit quite straight, and with a frail confidence
Assault the keyboard with a childish flourish!

Only to lose my place, or forget the key,
And almost doubt the very metronome
(Outside, the traffic, the laborers going home),
And still to bear on across Chopin or Brahms,
Stupid and wild with love equally for the storms
Of C# minor and the calms of C.

DONALD JUSTICE

"Your time is limited, so don't waste it living someone else's life. Don't be trapped by dogma—which is living with the results of other people's thinking. Don't let the noise of others' opinions drown out your own inner voice. And, most important, have the courage to follow your heart and intuition."

STEVE JOBS

"It takes courage to push yourself to places

that you have never been before . . . to test your limits . . .

to break through barriers. And the day came when the risk

it took to remain tight inside the bud was more painful that

the risk it took to blossom."

ANAÏS NIN

I HAVE BEEN
ABSOLUTELY TERRIFIED
EVERY MOMENT OF MY LIFE—
AND I'VE NEVER LET IT KEEP ME
FROM A SINGLE THING
I WANTED TO DO.

GEORGIA O'KEEFFE

COURAGE

IS NOT THE TOWERING OAK

THAT SEES STORMS COME AND GO;

IT IS THE FRAGILE BLOSSOM

THAT OPENS IN THE SNOW.

ALICE MACKENZIE SWAIM

AMONG CHILDREN

I walk among the rows of bowed heads—
the children are sleeping through fourth grade
so as to be ready for what is ahead,
the monumental boredom of junior high
and the rush forward tearing their wings
loose and turning their eyes forever inward.
These are the children of Flint, their fathers
work at the spark plug factory or truck
bottled water in 5 gallon sea-blue jugs
to the widows of the suburbs. You can see
already how their backs have thickened,
how their small hands, soiled by pig iron,
leap and stutter even in dreams. I would like
to sit down among them and read slowly
from The Book of Job until the windows
pale and the teacher rises out of a milky sea
of industrial scum, her gowns streaming

with light, her foolish words transformed
into song, I would like to arm each one
with a quiver of arrows so that they might
rush like wind there where no battle rages
shouting among the trumpets, Hal Ha!
How dear the gift of laughter in the face
of the 8 hour day, the cold winter mornings
without coffee and oranges, the long lines
of mothers in old coats waiting silently
where the gates have closed. Ten years ago
I went among these same children, just born,
in the bright ward of the Sacred Heart and leaned
down to hear their breaths delivered that day,
burning with joy. There was such wonder
in their sleep, such purpose in their eyes
dosed against autumn, in their damp heads
blurred with the hair of ponds, and not one
turned against me or the light, not one
said, I am sick, I am tired, I will go home,
not one complained or drifted alone,

unloved, on the hardest day of their lives.

Eleven years from now they will become

the men and women of Flint or Paradise,

the majors of a minor town, and I

will be gone into smoke or memory,

so I bow to them here and whisper

all I know, all I will never know.

PHILIP LEVINE

ONLY WHEN WE ARE
NO LONGER AFRAID
DO WE BEGIN TO LIVE.

DOROTHY THOMPSON

KEEP AWAY FROM PEOPLE WHO

TRY TO BELITTLE YOUR AMBITIONS.

SMALL PEOPLE ALWAYS DO THAT,

BUT THE REALLY GREAT

MAKE YOU FEEL THAT YOU, TOO,

CAN BECOME GREAT.

MARK TWAIN

"The terrorists thought that they would change our aims and stop our ambitions, but nothing changed in my life except this: weakness, fear and hopelessness died; strength, power and courage were born."

MALALA YOUSAFZAI

> "AS SOON AS WE ACCEPT LIFE'S MOST TERRIFYING dreadfulness, at the risk of perishing from it . . . then an intuition of blessedness will open up for us. . . . Whoever does not, sometime or other, give his full consent, his full and *joyous* consent, to the dreadfulness of life, can never take possession of the unutterable abundance and power of our existence."
>
> RAINER MARIA RILKE

Joseph Luzzi

COURAGE COMES to us through many different channels. Some of us can rely on well-honed courage, already put to the test. For others, it is a burst of unexpected courage that takes us completely off guard. Many wait and hope to be more courageous in times that deeply challenge them. And some, like Joseph Luzzi and others in the grip of mourning, grief, or depression, struggle to actively seek out the sources for the courage they need to pass through times of great tragedy.

Our culture rarely grants us the time we need to fully explore grief and find the courage to go on. We are often made to feel that we need to apologize for grief, especially when it doesn't go away according to some socially acceptable timetable. The story of

Joseph Luzzi is one of a man who turned to a most unusual source of inspiration. He allowed himself to *not* be okay for the time it took to experience the stillness and deep emotion that was necessary for healing to occur.

On an ordinary-seeming morning in November 2007, Joe, a professor at Bard College, was teaching his class in Italian literature when security guards arrived to inform him that his wife, who was eight and a half months pregnant with their first child, had been in a serious car accident. Standing in the hospital several hours later, he found himself both a widower and the father of a newborn baby girl. His despair was for his lost wife, their lost life together, and his complete inability to discern how to fulfill the new role of father. Not only was the despair overwhelming, but there seemed no possible avenue out. He was paralyzed by grief and overwhelmed by fear. He knew nothing of being a parent, let alone a single parent of a newborn. And he had never had to create and embark on a wholly new life with no warning at all. In a flash, he was on the hunt for the courage he needed.

Returning to his childhood home in Rhode Island, where his family embraced him and his new daughter, Isabel, allowed Joe the freedom to explore the true nature of grief, love, and parenthood, and search for the courage to step into the next chapter of his life. As he navigated the following months and years, his search turned more and more toward sources of personal inspiration that might come to his aid. He had read, studied, and taught the work of Dante for decades. He was as familiar with every verse of *The Divine Comedy* as one could be. Until this moment in his life, he had seen it as a towering work of art. Now he turned to Dante's words to provide the courage for a passage out of darkness that began with the opening lines of *The Divine Comedy*: "In the middle of the journey of our life, I came to myself, in a dark wood."

Dante's 14,000-line epic poem about the soul's journey through the underworld provided the road map Joe was looking for to come through his own version of hell—from the Inferno to the Purgatory of healing and finally to the Paradise of rediscovered love. "Studying Dante allowed me to climb out of my grief and mourning and find something magical," he says. In his years of struggle, he continually turned to Dante, taking each line as a wise guide. As his pain gradually began to ease, he took comfort in knowing that, in Dante's words, "you may visit the Underworld but you cannot live there."

Acknowledging that "all grief stories are essentially love stories," Joe felt the power of love giving him the courage he needed: "It was love that landed me in the dark wood to begin with, and only love could lead me out." Love of family and friends, but especially the inspiration of great and wise literature.

We all can acknowledge the power of artistic inspiration, whether we find it in painting, music, literature, poetry, or any other form. While many of us turn to great works for solace in difficult times, we rarely speak of this particular form of inspiration as a source of courage. It is generally a softer comfort that we look for in inspired art. But, for Joe Luzzi, it was courage he found. As he writes in his memoir, *In a Dark Wood: What Dante Taught Me About Grief, Healing, and the Mysteries of Love,* "In *The Divine Comedy,* courage was born from the belief that literature can transform you through 'lungo studio e grande amore' [long study and great love] and, in surrendering to beautiful writing, we begin what an astute reader of Dante, the poet Keats, called soul-making: how we must face a 'World of Pains and troubles' in order to realize our true selves and our full humanity."

Joe's grief was over lost love and, ultimately, the courage to love again brought him back to life. His daughter proved to be his first teacher of renewed love. Buoyed by her love and knowing intuitively that time and inspiration were going to be his twin healers, Joe emerged in the sunlight of new love and life. Now happily remarried, with a young son and flourishing writing career, he traces his renewal to the inspiring courage that he drew from the life and work of a great writer of the thirteenth century.

"The artist is extremely lucky who is presented

with the worst possible ordeal which will not actually kill him.

At that point, he is in business."

JOHN BERRYMAN

HE HAS NOT LEARNED
THE FIRST LESSON OF LIFE
WHO DOES NOT EVERY DAY
SURMOUNT A FEAR.

RALPH WALDO EMERSON

EITHER LIFE ENTAILS COURAGE,

OR IT CEASES TO BE LIFE.

E. M. FORSTER

CREATIVITY

REQUIRES THE COURAGE

TO LET GO OF CERTAINTIES.

ERICH FROMM

TOUCHED BY AN ANGEL

We, unaccustomed to courage
exiles from delight
live coiled in shells of loneliness
until love leaves its high holy temple
and comes into our sight
to liberate us into life.

Love arrives
and in its train come ecstasies
old memories of pleasure
ancient histories of pain.
Yet if we are bold,
love strikes away the chains of fear
from our souls.

We are weaned from our timidity
In the flush of love's light
we dare be brave
And suddenly we see
that love costs all we are
and will ever be.
Yet it is only love
which sets us free.

MAYA ANGELOU

"I had insecurities and fears like everybody does . . . but I was interested in the parts of me that struggled with those things."

PHILIP SEYMOUR HOFFMAN

LIFE SHRINKS
OR EXPANDS
IN PROPORTION TO ONE'S COURAGE.

ANAÏS NIN

PERFECT COURAGE

IS TO DO WITHOUT WITNESSES

WHAT ONE WOULD BE CAPABLE

OF DOING WITH THE WORLD

LOOKING ON.

FRANCOIS DE LA ROCHEFOUCAULD

ALL THE BRIGHT COURAGE

Not naked on the mountain were you reared
By wolf and weather, bramble-scratched and lean;
Privation has not made your senses keen
Since hunger is a thing you have always feared.
With fire, food and shelter you have cheered
A pampered body. What does courage mean
To one untried by danger? You have been
Safe and adventureless till love appeared.
Love is a ruthless bandit—may he shatter
The wall that bricks you snugly in content!
And though he wound and rob you, what shall it matter?
Accept his challenge. Who can circumvent
Death, collecting in person somewhat later
All the bright courage that you never spent!

Marjorie Allen Seiffert

Acknowledgments

A BEAUTIFUL CIRCLE of friends and colleagues went into the making of this book. Boundless thanks go to the wonderful team at Wisdom who believed in the book from the beginning and gave it their immensely thoughtful care and expertise—Tim McNeill, Laura Cunningham, Ben Gleason, Kestrel Slocombe, Lydia Anderson, and editor extraordinaire Josh Bartok. I am also beyond grateful to Gopa for the beautiful design of both this book and my previous book, *Inspiring Generosity.*

I am grateful beyond all words to the many remarkable individuals I interviewed for this book and am honored to include the stories of so many inspiring people who helped me reach a new understanding of courage. I am especially indebted to all those who put me in touch with some of the inspiring people whose stories I tell here. Leslie Thomas, Winnie Nazarko, Bryan Nurnberger, Caroline Wheeler, James Lescesne, Tara Brach and Koshin Paley Ellison made especially helpful introductions. Still others directed me to some of the poetry that you see here. Stephanie Wortman and Rob Forman introduced me to several contemporary poems I would likely not have known. Koshin alerted me to the magnificent Victoria Redel poem "Bedecked" during a dharma talk he gave in the summer of 2015. Michelle Gillett was an invaluable sounding board for the poems I selected as well as having suggested the Deborah Digges poem. My early attempts at writing in Michelle's workshops in 2005 undoubtedly laid the groundwork for the two books I have now written.

This book would simply not exist without the expertise and generosity of my writing partner Tresca Weinstein who always knew just the right word, skillfully straightened out my rather singular way of handling files, and spent a good deal of time keeping me out of trouble.

I am grateful for the daily inspiration of the many dharma teachers in my life, most especially those who call Barre, Massachusetts, home. It was their teachings more than anything else that led me to this exploration of what makes a courageous life.

I am thankful every day for my friends and colleagues who share reading and writing lives with me as well as joy in the written word and its power to inspire.

Poetry Permissions

Index of Names

About the Author

BARBARA BONNER started her professional life as an art historian, moving on to leadership positions at three New York City museums. She later served as Vice President of Bennington College and the Kripalu Center for Yoga and Health. She now has her own consulting practice focused on helping nonprofits transform their philanthropic support. Committed to a life in philanthropy, she has served on ten nonprofit boards and has started a fund to serve women with cancer in her region. She is currently board chair at the Barre Center for Buddhist Studies. A perennial student of contemplative traditions and yoga and avid gardener, she lives in a converted barn in the Berkshire hills of western Massachusetts. She is also the author of *Inspiring Generosity*.

Also Available from Wisdom Publications

Inspiring Generosity
Barbara Bonner

"I am amazed every day by the stories of people around the world who give of themselves to help others. *Inspiring Generosity* is a beautiful book."—President Bill Clinton

Daily Doses of Wisdom
A Year of Buddhist Inspiration
Josh Bartok

"100% organic healing Dharma. Effective for major and minor ailments of the heart."
—Kate Wheeler, editor of *The State of Mind Called Beautiful*

The Compassionate Life
His Holiness the Dalai Lama

"This sorely needed prescription for sanity and kindness in the world is unbelievably simple and unbelievably important, and therefore a practice worthy of our wholehearted commitment."—Jon Kabat-Zinn, author of *Wherever You Go, There You Are*

Saying Yes to Life
(Even the Hard Parts)
Ezra Bayda with Josh Bartok
Foreword by Thomas Moore

"Astonishing."—*Spirituality & Health*

Now!
The Art of Being Truly Present
Jean Smith

"Every saying in this book is a good tool for meditation."—*Eastern Horizon*

Kindfulness
Ajahn Brahm

"In a stroke of genius, Ajahn Brahm turns mindfulness into kindfulness, a practice that opens our hearts to others as well as to ourselves." —Toni Bernhard, author of *How to Be Sick*

Like a Yeti Catching Marmots
A Little Treasury of Tibetan Proverbs
Pema Tsewang, Shastri

"A treasure for Tibetans and English-speaking Westerners alike . . . This book can find a welcome spot in the center of any home."—*Mandala*

About Wisdom Publications

Wisdom Publications is the leading publisher of classic and contemporary Buddhist books and practical works on mindfulness. To learn more about us or to explore our other books, please visit our website at wisdompubs.org or contact us at the address below.

Wisdom Publications
199 Elm Street
Somerville, MA 02144 USA

We are a 501(c)(3) organization, and donations in support of our mission are tax deductible.

Wisdom Publications is affiliated with the Foundation for the Preservation of the Mahayana Tradition (FPMT).